普通高等教育"十一五"国家级规划教材
高职高专规划教材

实用会计英语
PRACTICAL ACCOUNTING ENGLISH

第3版

主　编　何妙婕　郭　梅　郭丽芳
副主编　李伊泠　邓满秀
参　编　尹平娥　王　军

机械工业出版社

本书共分10个教学单元，每个单元均包含专题故事、国际背景知识、精读课文、国际视野、单词与词组注释、课后习题以及阅读材料。所选内容题材涉及会计总论、账户与复式记账、流动资产、非流动资产、负债、所有者权益、收入、费用和利润、资产负债表、利润表、现金流量表。本书充分体现了高等职业教育的特色，理论内容以"必需、够用"为度，突出了实用性。

本书是普通高等教育"十一五"国家级规划教材之一，可作为高职高专院校财务会计类专业师生的教材及参考用书，也可作为各类会计从业人员的参考用书。

图书在版编目（CIP）数据

实用会计英语/何妙婕，郭梅，郭丽芳主编. —3版. —北京：机械工业出版社，2018.12

高职高专规划教材

ISBN 978 - 7 - 111 - 61712 - 9

Ⅰ.①实… Ⅱ.①何… ②郭… ③郭… Ⅲ.①会计-英语-高等职业教育-教材 Ⅳ.①F23

中国版本图书馆CIP数据核字（2018）第297502号

机械工业出版社（北京市百万庄大街22号 邮政编码100037）
策划编辑：孔文梅 责任编辑：孔文梅 董宇佳
责任校对：张 薇 封面设计：鞠 杨
责任印制：孙 炜
保定市中画美凯印刷有限公司印刷
2019年5月第3版·第1次印刷
184mm×260mm·12.75印张·338千字
0001 - 3000册
标准书号：ISBN 978 - 7 - 111 - 61712 - 9
定价：35.00元

凡购本书，如有缺页、倒页、脱页，由本社发行部调换

电话服务 网络服务
服务咨询热线：010-88379833 机 工 官 网：www.cmpbook.com
读者购书热线：010-68326294 机 工 官 博：weibo.com/cmp1952
 教育服务网：www.cmpedu.com
封底无防伪标均为盗版 金 书 网：www.golden-book.com

第3版前言

Preface

本书是普通高等教育"十一五"国家级规划教材、高职高专规划教材,自2007年出版以来获得了众多读者的厚爱。本书旨在使学生迅速掌握会计英语通用词汇和西方财务会计基本知识,掌握纯正的会计英语表达,提高使用英语处理会计工作的能力。

全书的内容安排如下:

(1) Study Objectives(学习目标)。每章的开头列出了本章的学习目标,提示读者在学习本章后应达到的要求。

(2) Feature Story(专题故事)。每一章都先介绍一篇与本章内容相关的专题故事,以提起读者的好奇心和学习兴趣。

(3) International Background Information(国际背景知识)。此部分主要介绍与本章内容相关的国际财务会计知识与规定,主要参照 Generally Accepted Accounting Principles(GAAP)(公认会计原则)、International Financial Reporting Standards(IFRS)(国际财务报告准则)。

(4) Text(课文)。每篇课文分为若干小节,以专题文章的形式介绍西方财务会计的基本知识。文章中的新词汇以旁注的方式标出,以便读者阅读学习。

(5) International Insight(国际视野)。介绍国际上不同国家各自特殊的具体的会计处理方法和规定,注重知识性与趣味性的有机结合。

(6) Notes(注释)。对于章节中的难词、难句,在该小节后配有中文注释。

(7) Assignment(习题)。习题以单项选择题、判断题和实务题为主,以使"教、学、做"一体化,帮助读者及时复习本课的重点内容和会计知识,训练语言能力,进而学会举一反三,运用会计英语知识进行会计业务处理。习题的参考答案收录在附录中。

(8) Reading Material(阅读材料)。每章后都有阅读材料和练习,对于学有余力的读者可作为课文的拓展阅读,进行进一步的学习研究。

(9) Appendix(附录)。附录中包括了习题的参考答案、课文的参考译文,以及专业词汇表,以方便读者学习。

本版在第2版的基础上进行了全面修订,增加了"国际背景知识"和"国际视野"版块,丰富了习题内容。

本次修订由广州航海学院何妙婕老师负责。在编写及修订过程中参考了国内外学者的成果和相关网站的资料,特别是美国、加拿大和澳大利亚现行的会计教材,编者在此表示衷心的感谢。由于时间仓促和编者水平有限,本书难免存在疏漏和不妥之处,敬请广大读者提出宝贵意见和建议。

为方便教学,本书配备了电子课件等教学资源。凡选用本书作为教材的教师均可登录机械工业出版社教育服务网 www.cmpedu.com 免费下载。如有问题请致电 010-88379375,联系营销人员,QQ:945379158。

编 者

第2版前言
Preface

本书第1版自2007年6月出版以来，得到了众多读者的厚爱，很多高职院校的师生对本教材给予了中肯的评价。在肯定本书的同时，他们也指出了书中所存在的各种错误和不足，提出了许多建设性意见。为了更好地满足读者对会计英语学习的需要，编者对本书进行了修订。

本次修订以财政部2007年1月1日实施的新企业会计准则为依据，保持了第1版的基本结构、内容体系和风格特点，在此基础上删除了部分过时的内容，使用了新的术语，并对所有资料和数据进行了更新，同时对一些重要的基本理论或知识点加以充实，以便读者更好地理解和学习本教材。

整体而言，第2版保留了原书的特色，编排新颖独特，使用方便；内容深入浅出，难易适度；语言清晰易懂。

本次修订由湖北交通职业技术学院郭梅、郭丽芳老师负责。教材修订具体分工为：李伊泠老师修订第1、2章，邓满秀老师修订第3、4章，刘悦老师修订第5章，郭梅老师修订第6章，郭丽芳老师修订第7、8、9章，尹平娥、王军老师修订第10章。

编 者

第1版前言
Preface

　　为适应我国加入 WTO 后经济发展的新形势，根据高职高专院校学生培养目标和要求，我们参阅了大量国内外会计专业文献，编写了这本实用会计英语教材。希望通过对本书的学习，读者能了解国内外最新的会计信息和案例，理解必需的会计英语专业知识，掌握一定的专业英语词汇，达到认知并使用英语处理常规会计业务、获取所需信息的目的。本书选取了具有针对性、实用性和可操作性的国内外素材和案例，力图使其成为"教师好教，学生易学"的实用型专业教材。

　　本书在编写过程中突出了以下特点：

　　（1）从学生的接受能力出发，选取的专业教学内容难易适中，有效地结合了会计专业和英语语言的特点，充分体现了培养高职高专应用型人才的特点。

　　（2）全书的编排新颖独特，使用方便。学习目标、引导案例、课文与单词的分栏排列便于学生学习；课后的练习侧重于培养学生用英语处理日常会计业务的实际操作能力；课后阅读提供了丰富的与篇章主题相关的英文资料。

　　本书由湖北交通职业技术学院郭梅、郭丽芳老师任主编，广东交通职业技术学院李伊泠老师、长沙大学邓满秀老师为副主编。武汉大学牟杨教授为本书的主审。教材编写具体分工为：李伊泠老师编写第1、2、7章，邓满秀老师编写第3、4、5章，郭梅老师编写第6章，郭丽芳老师编写第8章，王军老师编写第9章，尹平娥老师编写第10章。

　　本书的出版得到了机械工业出版社的大力支持和帮助，在此表示衷心的感谢。

　　由于时间仓促和编者水平有限，书中难免有错误和不当之处，敬请广大读者提出宝贵意见，以便今后修改。

编　者

目 录
Contents

第 3 版前言
第 2 版前言
第 1 版前言

Unit 1　General Introduction to Accounting ·············· 001

1.1　Origin and Development of Accounting ············· 002
1.2　Economic Entity ············· 006
1.3　Accounting Assumptions ············· 008
1.4　Quality Requirements of Accounting Information ············· 009
● Assignment ············· 012
● Reading Material ············· 013

Unit 2　Accounts and Double-Entry ··· 015

2.1　Account Titles and Accounts ············· 018
2.2　Accounting Elements and Accounting Equation ············· 021
2.3　Double Entry ············· 024
2.4　Accounting Cycle ············· 026
● Assignment ············· 029
● Reading Material ············· 031

Unit 3　Current Assets ·············· 032

3.1　Cash ············· 034
3.2　Receivables ············· 039
3.3　Inventories ············· 042
● Assignment ············· 044
● Reading Material ············· 047

Unit 4　Non-Current Assets ·············· 050

4.1　Long-Term Investments ············· 052
4.2　Property, Plant and Equipment ············· 054
4.3　Intangible Assets ············· 058

● Assignment ············· 060
● Reading Material ············· 063

Unit 5　Liabilities ·············· 066

5.1　Current Liabilities ············· 068
5.2　Long-Term Liabilities ············· 071
● Assignment ············· 074
● Reading Material ············· 076

Unit 6　Owners' Equity ·············· 079

6.1　Capital Stock ············· 080
6.2　Retained Earnings ············· 084
● Assignment ············· 085
● Reading Material ············· 087

Unit 7　Revenues, Expenses and Profits ·············· 089

7.1　Revenues ············· 091
7.2　Expenses ············· 093
7.3　Profits ············· 095
● Assignment ············· 097
● Reading Material ············· 099

Unit 8　Balance Sheet ·············· 101

8.1　Concept of the Balance Sheet ············· 103
8.2　Contents and Formats of the Balance Sheet ············· 105
8.3　How to Prepare the Balance Sheet ············· 107
● Assignment ············· 111
● Reading Material ············· 113

Unit 9　**Income Statement** ············· 116

9.1　Concept of the Income Statement ································· 117

9.2　Contents and Formats of the Income Statement ······················· 118

9.3　How to Prepare the Income Statement ································· 121

● Assignment ································ 123

● Reading Material ····························· 126

Unit 10　**Statement of Cash Flows** ······· 128

10.1　Concept of the Statement of Cash Flows ································ 129

10.2　Contents and Formats of the Statement of Cash Flows ················· 131

10.3　How to Prepare the Statement of Cash Flows ························· 133

● Assignment ································ 137

● Reading Material ····························· 139

APPENDIX ································· 141

Appendix Ⅰ　参考答案 ·············· 141

Appendix Ⅱ　课文参考译文 ········· 148

Appendix Ⅲ　专业词汇表 ············ 184

参考文献 ··································· 196

Unit 1　General Introduction to Accounting

Study Objectives

After studying this unit, you should be able to:
- Explain what accounting is.
- Explain the history of accounting.
- Identify users and uses of accounting.
- Explain the accounting assumption.
- Understand the working principles of accounting.

Feature Story

　　There is a popular accounting joke in Spain. An accountant was walking in the countryside when he found a shepherd who had a lot of sheep. The accountant said to the shepherd, "Listen, I can guess how many sheep you have." The shepherd started laughing, "Oh, dear! I have a lot of sheep. You will not be able to guess how many there are." "Let's make a bet. If I figure out how many sheep you have, you need to give me one of your sheep. If I can't, I will pay you $100." "OK, how many are there?" "There are exactly 1,354 sheep." The shepherd was shocked, "Incredible! I really have 1,354 sheep. Well, I'm a man of my word, take one." "Oh, I choose this one," said the accountant and he took one. "Wait for a moment, sir," said the shepherd. "Let's do another bet: if I guess right what your job is, you will give me back my sheep, and if I don't, you can take another one." "OK." "You are an accountant." "Oh, God! That's true. But, how do you know it?" "Give me back my sheep, and then I will tell you."

　　Do you know why the accountant knows the exact number of the sheep? How does the shepherd know the accountant's job? What is accounting?

　　In this unit, we'll introduce the real meaning of accounting, which includes the origin and development of accounting, accounting entity and accounting principles.

International Background Information

Accounting Standards

The main controversy in setting accounting standards is, "Whose rules should we play by, and what should they be?" The answer is not immediately clear because the users of financial accounting statements have both coinciding and conflicting needs for information of various types. To meet these needs, and to satisfy the fiduciary reporting responsibility of management, a single set of general-purpose financial statements is prepared. These statements are expected to present fairly, clearly and completely the financial operations of the enterprises.

As a result, the accounting profession has attempted to develop a set of standards that are generally accepted and universally practiced. Without these standards, each enterprise would have to develop its own standards, and readers of financial statements would have to familiarize themselves with every company's peculiar accounting and reporting practices. It would be almost impossible to prepare statements that could be compared.

This common set of standards and procedures is called generally accepted accounting principles (GAAP). The term "generally accepted" means either an authoritative accounting rule-making body has established a principle of reporting in a given area or over time a given practice has been accepted as appropriate because of its universal application.

会计标准

n. 企业
财务报表

公认会计原则

1.1 Origin and Development of Accounting

Function of Accounting

Today, many people are proudly taking up accounting as a career. Actually, nearly everyone practices accounting in one form or another on an almost daily basis. Accounting is a basic and vital element in every modern business. The bookkeeping method being used is involved in making a financial record of busi-

n. 会计，会计学

adj. 至关重要的/n. 簿记，记账/涉及，投入

ness transactions and in the preparation of statements concerning the assets, liabilities, and operating results of a business.

As the "language of business", accounting links decision makers with economic activities and (with) the results of their decisions. Since every investor, manager, and business decision maker needs a clear understanding of accounting terms and concepts, a nation's economy depends heavily upon the work of these accountants.

International Insight

The objectives of financial reporting differ across nations. Traditionally, the primary objective of accounting in many continental European nations and in Japan was conformity with the law. In contrast, Canada, the U.K., the Netherlands, and many other nations have shared the U.S. view that the primary objective is to provide information for investors.

Notes

The objectives of financial reporting differ across nations.
不同国家的财务报告的目标是不一样的。

Ancient Accounting

The history of accounting is as old as civilization. It is among the most important professions in economic and cultural development. The seeds of accounting were most-likely first sown in the city of Babylon around 4000 B.C. when record keeping probably began in this civilized area.[1] Babylon prided itself as the city of commerce; moreover, Babylonians were characterized as meticulous bookkeepers. Thus, they were big on recording things in detailed accounts.[2] Their major purpose for keeping such accurate books centered on uncovering losses triggered by fraud and lack of efficiency.

Unlike most other modern professions, there are no household names among the accounting innovators. In fact, no names survived before the Italian Renaissance. The first systematic presentation of record keeping appeared in 1494, two years after Columbus discovered America, and was called "double entry". The author Luca Pacioli, a Franciscan friar, is referred to as "the father of accounting".[3] His book, *Summary of arithmetic*, *geometry*, *proportions and proportionality*, is one of the most important books on mathematics and has had an enormous impact on the field of accounting ever since.

The first known English book on the science of accounting was published in London by John Gouge in 1543. It was described as a profitable instrument to learn the order of the bookkeeping records, called Debit and Credit. After that, in 1635, a book named *The Merchant's Mirror* was published. In the book, the author cited quotations of Latin book-keeping terms which were used in ancient times. And he explained that, "One side of their book was used for Debt, the other for Credit, as is manifest in a certain place." The book is a very complete treatise on accounting science. It was beautifully prepared and contains elaborate explanations to prove that the science was highly appreciated in the 17th century.

Accounting in Modern Times

Although accounting dates back to ancient civilizations, its importance to society became fairly great after the industrial revolution. The 19th century industrial revolution generated the need for large amounts of capital to finance the enterprises that supplanted individual craftsmanship. The use of machinery in turning out many identical products gave rise to the need to determine the cost of a large volume of machine-made products instead of the cost of a relatively small number of individually handcrafted products.[4] The specialized field of cost accounting emerged to meet the need for the analysis of various costs and for recording techniques.

As manufacturing enterprises became larger and more complex and as competition among manufacturers increased, more sophisticated accounting concepts were needed to supply management with analytical techniques for measuring the efficiency of current operations and in planning for future operations. This trend was accelerated in the 20th century by the advent of the electronic computer.

Nowadays, accounting is in an age of rapid transition. Accounting is moving away from its traditional procedural base—encompassing record keeping and such related work as the preparation of budgets and final accounts towards a role which emphasizes its social importance. The changing environment has not only extended the boundaries of accounting but also created a problem in defining the scope of the subject. For this reason, the origin and development of accounting should receive more attention today. This will provide a better understanding of the influence that accounting has had on society and the basis for what accountants do today.

n. 制造业者，厂商
adj. 久经世故的，复杂的

离开

n. 预算

n. 边界，分界线

International Insight

Parties Involved in Standards Setting

A number of organizations are instrumental in the development of financial accounting standards in the United States. Three major organizations are as follows.
1. Securities and Exchange Commission (SEC) 证券交易委员会
2. American Institute of Certified Public Accountants (AICPA) 美国注册会计师协会
3. Financial Accounting Standards Board (FASB) 财务会计准则委员会

Notes

1. The seeds of accounting were most-likely first sown in the city of Babylon around 4000 B. C. when record keeping probably began in this civilized area.
   这是一个比喻句，将会计的起源比喻成种子的萌芽。该句的意思是：
   会计学极有可能产生于公元前大约 4 000 年的巴比伦，这里最早开始记录人类文明。

2. Thus, they were big on recording things in detailed accounts.

be big on 喜爱，该句的意思是：

他们喜欢将事情详细记录在账目上。

3. The author Luca Pacioli, a Franciscan friar, is referred to as "the father of accounting".

提出者 Luca Pacioli，一位圣方济会修道士，被称为"会计学之父"。

4. The use of machinery in turning out many identical products gave rise to the need to determine the cost of a large volume of machine-made products instead of the cost of a relatively small number of individually handcrafted products.

本句为带有多层定语的复合句，其简化形式是：The use gave rise to the need。该句的意思是：

机器的运用能够生产大量同种产品，由此产生了计算大批量产品成本的需要，而不是计算小规模个体手工产品。

1.2　Economic Entity

An economic entity is the particular unit for which the accounting serves. Economic entities can be divided into the following types according to its legal status.

Sole Proprietorship Enterprises

A sole proprietorship enterprise is a single-owner business and the simplest form of business entity. The individual proprietor retains sole control over the management and development of the business. The administrative costs are minimal. However, a sole proprietorship enterprise is also the most restrictive form of business equity. All the business debts and liabilities are the owner's personal obligations. He is personally responsible for the business's contracts, taxes, and legal liabilities arising from the misconduct of employees during their employment. The financing options of a sole proprietorship enterprise are limited. The owner may have a difficult time obtaining debt financing, unless to some extent he can pledge personal assets as security for a loan.

独资（经营）制
n. 所有者，经营者

管理费用
adj. 限制性的

n. 不正当的行为

n. 筹措资金，融资

普通合伙制

General Partnership Enterprises

A general partnership enterprise is created by written agreement, and the relationship of the partners is governed by that understanding. Partners typically agree to share the tangible assets and intangible assets of the partnership enterprise. In addition, each individual partner shares the profit and loss of the business according to the agreed-upon allocation of partnership enterprise interests. The partners raise equity funds through their own capital contributions. When adding a new partner, or restructuring the ownership interests of the existing partners, parters shall take corresponding rights and interests according to their capital contributions.

A general partnership enterprise has unlimited personal liability for business liabilities. Each partner bears personal financial liability for the contract and tort debts of the business. Furthermore, most partnership enterprise arrangements restrict the partners' rights to withdraw from the partnership enterprise or to transfer their ownership interests.

Obtaining financing, especially long-term financing, is often difficult for small partnership enterprises.

Limited Liability Partnership Enterprises

A limited liability partnership enterprise is similar to a general partnership enterprise in certain aspects and similar to a corporation in others. A limited liability partnership enterprise is a business relationship form often available only for certain occupations, such as lawyers or CPAs[1], with one or more of the partners having only limited liability for partnership debts and obligations. The price for this liability protection is a limitation on participation in management.

Corporation

A corporation is a legal entity created under a particular business statute. A corporation is regarded, in law, as having a personality and existence entirely distinct from that of its owners. Accordingly, shareholders are generally not liable for corporate obligations. Corporations offer an even greater opportunity to bring together large amounts of capital from multiple owners. However, there are some disadvantages of this form, such as the huge expense and administrative burden of maintaining the formalities of corporate structure, <u>double taxation of profits while operating, and double taxation of capital gains upon dissolution.</u> ²

Notes

1. A limited liability partnership enterprise is a business form often available only for certain occupations, such as lawyers or CPAs…
   CPA = Certified Public Accountants 注册会计师。该句意思为：
   有限责任合伙企业这种经营方式通常只用于某些特定的行业，如律师或注册会计师……

2. …double taxation of profits while operating, and double taxation of capital gains upon dissolution.
   这句是指企业赚取利润时，要缴纳企业所得税；而这些利润如果分配股利，个人还要缴纳个人所得税。这对于股东来说等于支付了双倍税额。

1.3　Accounting Assumptions

Accounting has evolved through time, and changed with the needs of society. As new types of transactions evolved in trade and commerce, accountants developed rules and practices for recording. The most fundamental concepts underlying the accounting are:

adj. 基础的

(1) Economic Entity Assumption

The economic entity assumption means that economic activity can be identified with a particular unit of accountability. A business is an entity that is separate and distinct from its owners, so the finances of the firm can not be co-mingled with the finances of the owners. Furthermore, the entity concept does not necessarily refer to a legal entity.

经济主体假设（我国称为会计主体假设）

(2) Going Concern Assumption

持续经营假设

The going concern assumption means that the business enterprise will have a long life. Most accounting methods are based on that the business enterprise is a continuing entity and will remain in operation into the foreseeable future.

adj. 可预知的

The going concern assumption applies in most business situations. Only where liquidation appears imminently is the assumption inapplicable.

(3) **Monetary Unit Assumption**

Financial accounting takes currency as its unit of measure under the assumption that the currency is stable.

> **International Insight**
>
> Due to their experiences with persistent inflation, several South American countries produce "constant currency" financial reports. Typically, a general price-level index is used to adjust for the effects of inflation.

货币计量假设

由于
财务报告
v. 调整
n. 通货膨胀

(4) **Periodicity Assumption**

The periodicity assumption implies that the economic activities of an enterprise can be divided into artificial time periods. Accounting periods may be a fiscal year, a quarter, or a month, commencing on first days thereof according to the Gregorian calendar.[1]

会计期间假设

1.4 Quality Requirements of Accounting Information

会计信息质量要求

> **International Insight**
>
> In Switzerland, Germany, Korea, and other nations, capital is provided to businesses primarily by large banks. Creditors have very close ties to firms and can obtain information directly from them. Creditors do not need to rely on publicly available information, and financial information is focused on creditor protection. This process of capital allocation, however, is changing.

n. 债权人
n. 束缚,关系/n. 公司/v. 获得

(1) **Objectivity Principle**

The accounting records and financial reports must be based on financial and economic transactions as they actually take place. According to the objectivity principle, the accounting records from which the periodic accounting statements are prepared must be objective and verifiable; they must be maintained in such a way that the individual bias or personal opinion of the accountant does not

客观性原则

n. 偏见,偏爱

influence the accounting process.

(2) Comparability Principle

Accounting records and financial statements shall be prepared according to stipulated accounting methods, and accounting information of enterprises must be comparable and convenient to be analyzed.

(3) Pertinence Principle

Accounting information provided by an enterprise should be capable of reflecting the financial position, operating results and cash flows of the enterprise in order to meet the requirements of accounting information users.

(4) Timeliness Principle

The preparation of accounting records and financial reports must be conducted in a timely manner, and shall not be in advance or delayed.

(5) Full Disclosure Principle

Accounting records and financial reports shall be prepared in a clear and concise manner to facilitate understanding, examination and use. Financial reports must reflect comprehensively the financial position and operating results of an enterprise.

(6) Prudence Principle

The principle of prudence should be followed in reasonably determining the possible loss and expense. According to the principle, the accountant will recognize revenues and assets only when there is virtual certainty of an advantageous event occurring. This also means that suspected but uncertain losses should be anticipated. This principle is a prudent reaction to uncertainty and is adopted in order to ensure that adequate consideration is given to all inherent business risks.

International Insight

In Japan, assets are often undervalued and liabilities overvalued by companies. These practices reduce the demand for dividends and protect creditors in event of a default.

可比性原则

v. 规定,保证

相关性原则

及时性原则

明晰性原则(充分披露原则)

谨慎性原则

vt. 预期,预料

vt. 低估/高估负债
v. 减少
n. 股利/不履行偿债义务

Unit 1 General Introduction to Accounting

(7) Materiality Principle   重要性原则

An enterprise should assess the materiality of transactions or events in the process of accounting to determine the manner in which they should be accounted for. Material events should be accounted for in accordance with prescribed accounting treatments and procedures, and disclosed in the financial and accounting reports adequately and accurately.

v. 指示，规定

(8) Realization Principle   实质重于形式原则

An enterprise should account for transactions and events according to their economic substance and should not merely refer to their legal form.

International Insight

Qualitative Characteristics of Accounting Information[2]

The FASB has identified the qualitative characteristics of accounting information that distinguish better (more useful) information from inferior (less useful) information for decision making purposes:

◇ Decision makers (users) and understandability. Decision makers vary widely in the types of decisions they make, how they make decisions, the information they already possess or can obtain from other sources, and their ability to process the information. For information to be useful there must be a connection (linkage) between these users and the decisions they make. This link, understandability, is the quality of information that permits reasonably informed users to perceive its significance.

n. 可理解性

◇ Primary qualities: relevance and reliability. Relevance and reliability are the two primary qualities that make accounting information useful for decision making.

n. 相关性/*n.* 可靠性

◇ Secondary qualities: comparability and consistency. Information about an enterprise is more useful if it can be compared with similar information about another enterprise (comparability) and with similar information about the same enterprise at other points in time (consistency).

n. 可比性/*n.* 一致性

Notes

1. Accounting periods may be a fiscal year, a quarter, or a month, commencing on first days thereof according to the Gregorian calendar.

   Gregorian calendar 格列高利历，也就是公历。该句的意思是：

   会计期间可以为一个财政年度、一个季度或一个月，其起讫日期可采用公历日期。

2. Qualitative Characteristics of Accounting Information

   会计信息质量要求

   注：此段为 FASB（财务会计准则委员会）所规定的会计信息质量要求，与我国的八大会计信息质量要求稍有不同。

Assignment

I. Select the best answer for each of the following questions or uncompleted sentences.

(1) The basic functions of an accounting system include _____.

   A. interpreting and recording the effects of business transactions

   B. classifying the effects of similar transactions

   C. summarizing and communicating the information contained in the system

   D. A, B and C

(2) Accounting principles can be applied to the financial statements of which of the following? _____.

   A. Sole Proprietorship enterprises   B. Partnership enterprises

   C. Corporations   D. A, B and C

(3) The Realization Principle indicates that revenue usually should be recognized and recorded in the accounting record, _____.

   A. when goods are sold or services are rendered to customers

   B. when cash is collected from customers

   C. at the end of the accounting period

   D. only when the revenue can be matched by an equal dollar amount of expenses

(4) Which of the following concepts belongs to accounting assumption? _____.

   A. Conservatism   B. Monetary Unit

   C. Materiality   D. Consistency

(5) The Matching Principle: _____.

   A. applies only to situations in which a cash payment occurs before an expense is recognized

   B. applies only to situations in which a cash receipt occurs before revenue is recognized

   C. is used in accrual accounting to determine the proper period for recognition of expenses

   D. is used in accrual accounting to determine the proper period in which to recognize revenue

(6) The idea that a business be accounted for separately and independently from its owners is known as the _____.
   A. going concern assumption
   B. economic entity assumption
   C. monetary unit assumption
   D. periodicity assumption

(7) The accounting process is correctly sequenced as _____.
   A. identification, recording, communication
   B. identification, communication, recording
   C. recording, communication, identification
   D. communication, recording, identification

(8) Which of the following is the assumption that the economic activities of an enterprise can be divided into artificial time periods? _____.
   A. Going concern assumption
   B. Economic entity assumption
   C. Monetary unit assumption
   D. Periodicity assumption

Ⅱ. Mark the correct items by "√" and the wrong items by "×".

(1) Accounting is another word for bookkeeping. (   )
(2) Accounting provides financial information that is only useful to business management. (   )
(3) The accounting reporting period agrees to the calendar year. (   )
(4) Without the Consistency Principle, the comparisons which might be made and conclusions could mislead. (   )
(5) The accounting process generates financial reports for both "internal" and "external" users. (   )
(6) Decision makers are the users of accounting information. (   )

Reading Material

Careers in Accounting

Even though many changes in accounting have occurred over the past years, it continues to be a popular career choice for many students. Nowadays, there are two major fields of accounting activity. One is private accounting, and the other is public accounting.

More accountants are employed in private accounting than in any other field for its career opportunities have remained very stable. Any company, whether large or small, must prepare various financial records for both internal and external use. The world will always need accountants. Despite the recent instability in the world's financial markets, accounting graduates continue to find no difficulty in job hunting.

Private employers of accountants include manufacturers, wholesalers, retailers, and service firms. An accounting graduate can easily get a place in a company. He or she can either be a treasurer, who is in charge of funds, or be an accountant who inspects the financial records of individuals or business concerns and prepares financial and tax reports. Even on the lower levels, salaries for people with accounting training are usually good. And they are usually given the chance to move upward in the company, such as the Chief Financial Officer.

Public accountants are often referred to as CPAs. They work for public accounting firms, both small and large. The most important work for them is to audit financial statements for types of entities. The task of audit professionals, as the word implies, is to carefully and rigorously audit and document all the financial records and business transactions of their clients. The CPAs verify that all client accounting records reported publicly to shareholders are accurate, and that they abide by national accounting standards. They may also conduct compliance and operation audits for such entities.

Their ability to identify and solve unstructured problems in an unfamiliar setting and provide insightful consulting advice is a valued quality. Public accounting firms also provide a variety of services to their clients. CPAs are well-respected strategic business advisors and decision-makers. They usually act as consultants on many issues, including taxes and accounting.

CPAs receive fees for their services. Their income is usually higher than the private accountants. In the long-term, as long as your performance is strong, you can eventually become a partner in the firm. In fact, CPAs possess a wide scope of knowledge, competency and skills ranging from a strong understanding of accounting and business concepts to effective leadership and communication skills. A great many companies like to offer a fat salary to make them move into the top management positions.

In a word, accounting offers students lots of career options.

Exercises:

Match the Chinese expressions in Column B to the English ones in Column A.

A	B
(1) Private accountant	a 总会计师
(2) Public accountant	b 顾问
(3) Certified Public Accountant	c 出纳员
(4) Chief Financial Officer	d 私营企业会计
(5) Manufacturer	e 零售商
(6) Wholesaler	f 注册会计师
(7) Retailer	g 制造商
(8) Treasurer	h 首席财务官
(9) Finance Controller	i 批发商
(10) Consultant	j 公众会计

Unit 2　Accounts and Double-Entry

Study Objectives

After studying this unit, you should be able to:
- Describe the chart of accounts and recognize commonly used accounts.
- Define double-entry system and state the rules for double entry.
- State the steps in the accounting cycle.
- Apply the steps for transaction analysis and processing to simple transactions.

Feature Story

There's an old accounting joke. There was an accountant who worked in the same office for 50 years. Every day, the man came to work and did the same thing. He would sit down at his desk, unlock it, open the top left drawer and look inside and close it. Then he would open the top right drawer and look inside and close it. Once that routine was complete, he would again lock his desk and work all day. When he finally retired, his office mates rushed to his desk to see what was in those two top drawers. In the left one was a sign that said DEBIT, and in the right one was a sign that said CREDIT.

Why did the accountant mark the drawers with DEBIT and CREDIT? What is the meaning of that?

In this unit, we'll introduce the accounting system, including account titles and accounts, accounting elements, accounting equation, double-entry and accounting cycle. After reading it, you will understand the meaning of DEBIT and CREDIT in the story.

International Background Information

1. Accounting Information System

The system of collecting and processing transaction data and disseminating financial information to interested parties is known

会计信息系统

n. 交易

as the accounting information system. Accounting information systems vary widely from one business to another. Factors that shape these systems are the nature of the business and the transactions in which it engages the size of the firm, the volume of data to be handled, and the informational demands that managements and others place on the system.

A good accounting information system helps managements answer such questions as:

How much and what kind of debt is outstanding?

Are our sales higher this period than last?

What assets do we have?

What are our cash inflows and outflows?

Did we make a profit last period?

Are any of our product lines or divisions operating at a loss?

Can we safely increase our dividends to stockholders?

Is our rate of return on net assets increasing?

Many other questions can be answered when there is an efficient accounting system to provide the data. A well-devised accounting information system is beneficial for every business enterprise.

2. Basic Terminology

Financial accounting rests on a set of concepts for identifying, recording, classifying, and interpreting transactions and other events related to enterprises. It is important to understand the basic terminology employed in collecting accounting data.

- Event—a happening of consequence. An event generally is the source or cause of changes in assets, liabilities, and equity. Events may be external or internal.
- Transaction—an external event involving a transfer or exchange between two or more entities.
- Account—a systematic arrangement that shows the effect of transactions and other events on a specific asset or equity. A separate account is kept for each asset, liability, revenue, expense and for capital (owners' equity).

- Real and nominal accounts. Real (permanent) accounts are asset, liability and equity accounts; they appear on the balance sheet. Nominal (temporary) accounts are revenue, expense and dividend accounts; except for dividends, they appear on the income statement. Nominal accounts are periodically closed; real accounts are not.
- Ledger—the book (or computer printouts) containing the accounts. Each account usually has a separate page. A general ledger is a collection of all the asset, liability, owners' equity, revenue, and expense accounts. A subsidiary ledger contains the details related to a given general ledger account.
- Journal—the book of original entry where transactions and selected other events are initially recorded. Various amounts are transferred to the ledger from the book of original entry, the journal.
- Posting—the process of transferring the essential facts and figures from the book of original entry to the ledger accounts.
- Trial balance—a list of all open accounts in the ledgers and their balances. A trial balance taken immediately after all adjustments have been posted is called adjusted trial balance. A trial balance taken immediately after closing entries have been posted is designated as a post-closing or after-closing trial balance. A trial balance may be prepared at any time.
- Adjusting entries—entries made at the end of an accounting period to bring all accounts up to date on an accrual accounting basis so that correct financial statements can be prepared.
- Financial statements—statements that reflect the collection, tabulation, and final summarization of the accounting data. Four statements are involved: ①The balance sheet shows the financial condition of the enterprise at the end of a period. ②The income statement measures the results of oper-

ations during the period. ③The statement of cash flows reports the cash provided and used by operating, investing, and financing activities during the period. ④The statement of retained earnings reconciles the balance of the retained earnings account from the beginning to the end of the period.

- Closing entries—the formal process by which all nominal accounts are reduced to zero and the net income or net loss is determined and transferred to the owners' equity account; also known as "closing the ledger" "closing the books" or merely "closing".

Notes

The statement of retained earnings…
美国的财务报告中有一张专门报表用来反映留存收益，即留存收益表（the statement of retained earnings）。这张表中涉及了留存收益的期初、期末数及股利分配情况，但对留存收益的分拨情况没有披露。公司往往在资产负债表中对留存收益的分拨进行说明，一般是在"留存收益"项目后面加括号注明分拨的金额及用途。另外，在财务报告附注中也对分拨情况予以反映。

2.1 Account Titles and Accounts

An accounting system is comprised of accounting records (checkbooks, journals, ledgers, etc.) and a series of processes and procedures. The goal of the accounting system is to ensure that financial data and economic transactions are properly entered into the accounting records, and that financial reports necessary for management are prepared accurately and in a timely fashion. Traditionally, the accounting system includes the following components:

Chart of Accounts

The first step in setting up an accounting system for your business is deciding what you want to track. A chart of accounts is simply a list of the account titles and is kept by every business to record and follow specific entries. There are two parts in the chart of accounts. One is account number, and the other is account title. For most businesses, a four-number system will suffice, however, a six-number system is sometimes used for more complex businesses. For example:

Account number	Account Title
1001	Cash
1002	Cash in bank
100201	Cash in bank —Agricultural Bank of China

Accounts

Once an account has been established in the system, transactions originated on various source documents must be posted to the account.[1] An account is the basic storage unit for data in accounting for business transactions. It is a device used to provide a record of increase and decrease in each item that appears in a firm's financial statements. The management must be able to refer to these accounts so that it can study the company's financial history and plan for the future.

An account's simplified format is called a T-account because of its similarity to the letter T. The account title is written above the T-account. We label the left side of the T as "debit" and the right side as "credit". The debit side is abbreviated as "Dr.", and credit side is abbreviated as "Cr.". These can be illustrated graphically as follows:

Account Title	
Left or Debit Side (Dr.)	**Right or Credit Side** (Cr.)

Types of Accounts

1. General Ledger Accounts

The general ledger, sometimes known as the nominal ledger, is the main accounting record of a business. Every account that is on your chart of accounts will be included in your general ledger, which should be set up in the same order as the chart of accounts. The general ledger is a summary of all the transactions that occur in the company. It does not include every single accounting entry in a given period, but reflects a summary of all transactions made. It is usually divided into at least five main categories which generally include assets, liabilities, owners' equity, revenue and expenses.

The form of general ledger account should include the date, description and balance entries for each account. Shown as follow:

Account Title　　　　　　　　　　**Account No.** _____

Date	Description	Debit	Credit	Balance

Because each transaction debits one account and credits another, to an equal extent an accounting system will ensure that the general ledger account will always be in balance unless, for example, an account (sometimes called a T-account) is deleted or mis-specified. The balance sheet and the income statement are both derived from the general ledger. Because it is made up of accounts, the general ledger allows you to observe the impact of all the transactions affecting each account at any given time.

2. Subsidiary Ledger Accounts

Each subsidiary ledger account (SL) is identified with a general ledger account (GL) through the use of an attribute known as the account number.[2] This number establishes a relationship between the SL and GL account.

There are two possible types of GL/SL relationships.

- **One GL to One SL**: In this relationship, the balance in the GL account is updated by a single SL account. It provides details for the general ledger, to help the managers to know how the transactions affect the financial position of the account. In this case, the GL and the SL account usually have the same account name.

• **One GL to Many SLs**: In this relationship, several SL accounts update the same GL account. This structure is useful when the cash balance must be monitored at a higher level. For example, to monitor the detail of the bank deposit whose account title is "Cash in bank", we can establish several subsidiary ledger accounts, such as "Cash in bank — Agricultural Bank of China" "Cash in bank — Bank of China" and "Cash in bank — China Construction Bank".

Notes

1. Once an account has been established in the system, transactions originated on various source documents must be posted to the account.
   Once 引导的条件状语从句为虚拟语气，表示：一旦；一……就。该句的意思是：
   一旦会计系统的账户建立好之后，与各种经营活动相关的交易信息都必须反映在账户上。

2. Each subsidiary ledger account (SL) is identified with a general ledger account (GL) through the use of an attribute known as the account number.
   be identified with 以……著名；支持；联系在一起。该句的意思是：
   每一个明细分类账户（SL）都支持一个独立的总分类账户（GL），并通过采用账户代码表现出来。

2.2　Accounting Elements and Accounting Equation

To better understand the financial accountings, you need to know the accounting elements and accounting equation. What are accounting elements? Accounting elements are basic classification of accounting objectives, and embody the object of accounting practices. Assets, liabilities, owners' equity, revenues, expenses and profits are known as six accounting elements of a business enterprise. Among them, assets, liabilities and owners' equity reflect the financial position of the enterprise; revenues, expenses and profits reflect the management result of the enterprise.

会计要素

n. 分类

vt. 具体表达/会计核算

经营结果

Assets

Assets are economic resources, which are measurable by money value, and are owned or controlled by an enterprise, including all properties, rights as a creditor to others, and other rights. Assets are normally divided into current assets, long-term investments, fixed assets, intangible assets, deferred assets and other assets. Current assets refer to those assets that will be realized or consumed within one year after their acquisition, or within an operating cycle longer than a year. Long-term investments refer to the investments impossible or not intended to be realized within a year. Fixed assets refer to the assets whose useful life is over one year, whose unit value is above the prescribed criteria and original physical form remains during the process of utilization. Intangible assets refer to assets that will be used by an enterprise for a long term without material state. Deferred assets refer to all the expenses that could not be accounted totally as current profit or loss but should be periodically amortized in future years. Other assets refer to the assets except all the items mentioned above.

流动资产

长期投资

固定资产

无形资产

递延资产

v. 分期清偿

Liabilities

A liability is a debt borne by an enterprise, measured by money value, which will be paid to the creditor by using assets or services. This is in marked contrast to an asset which is something of value that you own. It is said, "Assets put cash in your pocket, and liabilities take cash out of your pocket." Liabilities are generally classified into current liabilities and long-term liabilities. Current liabilities refer to the debts which should be paid off within a year or an operating cycle longer than a year, including short-term loans payable, notes payable, accounts payable, advances from customers, accrued payroll, taxes payable, dividends payable, etc. Long-term liabilities refer to the debts which will be redeemed after a year or an operating cycle longer than a year, including long-term loans payable, bonds payable, long-term accounts payable, etc.

短期借款
应付票据/预收货款
应付股利
vt. 赎回

Owners' Equity

Owners' equity refers to the interest of the investors remaining in the net assets of an enterprise, including capital of the enterprise invested in by investors, capital reserve, surplus reserve,

所有者权益

资本公积/盈余公积

and undistributed profit retained in the enterprise etc. In a corporation, it is called shareholders' equity.

Revenues

Revenues refer to the financial inflows to an enterprise as a result of the sale of goods and services, and other business activities of the enterprise, including basic operating revenues and other operating revenues.

Expenses

Expenses refer to the outlays incurred by an enterprise in the course of production and operation, in the form of outflows or depletions of assets or incurrence of liabilities during a period. Increase in expenses will decrease owners' equity. Revenues and expenses are the subdivisions of Owners' Equity.

Profits

Profits are the operating results of an enterprise in an accounting period, including operating profits, net investment profits and net non-operating income. When revenues exceeds expenses, net income occurs, otherwise net loss occurs.

Accounting Equation

The relationship between the accounting elements can be expressed in a simple mathematical form known as the accounting equation.

Assets = Liabilities + Owners' Equity

Mathematically, the amount of total assets minus total liabilities is equal to the owners' equity. Since to be the net difference between assets and liabilities, owners' equity is also called net assets.

Initially, owners' equity is affected by capital contributions such as the issuance of capital stock. Once business operations commence, there will be income (revenues minus expenses, or gains minus losses) and perhaps additional capital contributions and withdrawals such as dividends.[1] At the end of a reporting period, these items will impact the owners' equity as follows:

Assets = Liabilities + Owners' Equity$_{beg}$ + (Revenues − Expenses)

Finally, this equation may be rearranged algebraically as follows:

adv. 用代数方法

Assets + Expenses = Liabilities + Owners' Equity$_{beg}$ + Revenues

This equation must be true, for any time period. If it is, then the accounts are said to be in balance. If the accounts are not in balance, an error has occurred.

Notes

1. Once business operations commence, there will be income (revenues minus expenses, or gains minus losses) and perhaps additional capital contributions and withdrawals such as dividends.
企业开始经营之后，就会出现收益（收入减去费用，或者所得减去损失），也可能出现新增资本，或因分配股利等而减少资本。

2. 会计恒等式：资产 = 负债 + 所有者权益（Assets = Liabilities + Owners' Equity）中的"所有者权益"变化是有规律的，它是年初的所有者权益数额加上本年的净利润，减去本年的净损失和发放股利后的数额。为了将会计六要素的关系都通过会计恒等式表示出来，会计恒等式可以变形为：资产=负债+年初所有者权益+（收入－费用），即 Assets = Liabilities + Owners' Equity$_{beg}$ + (Revenues − Expenses)。在本式中，资产、负债是当年资产负债表上的年末数；所有者权益是当年资产负债表上的年初数；收入、费用都是当年利润表上的发生数。

2.3 Double Entry

Definition of Double-Entry Accounting

Double entry bookkeeping is a method of recording transactions, which allows a check on accuracy of the recording. For examples:

(1) ABC Company makes an entry for paying its telephone bill like this:

    Administrative expenses $50
    (Increase the expense of debit)

    Cash $50
        (Decrease the asset of credit)
  (2) The telephone company would record the exact same transaction (from their side) like this:
    Cash $50
        (Increase the asset of debit)
            Prime operating revenue $50
                (Increase the revenue of credit)

Rules of Double-Entry Accounting

Rule 1. The Duality Rule

Every transaction has two effects. One is recorded as a debit in one account, and the other is recorded as a credit in another account. Debits must always equal credits. Because debits equal credits, double-entry accounting prevents some common book-keeping errors.

n. 二元性

Rule 2. The Directionality Rule

Most people think of credits as minus and debits as plus, but there are many account types working differently. To distinguish them, we have debit and credit accounts.

All the asset accounts and expense accounts are debit accounts, which mean they are positive numbers. In other words, an asset is a positive number in the system. The liability accounts are all credit accounts and they are negative numbers, but generally when you see them on the balance sheet, you don't see the minus sign. The owners' equity accounts and revenue accounts are considered as credit accounts. The expense accounts are all debit accounts.

减号

The following chart shows how debits and credits affect different types of accounts.

Account Type	Debit	Credit
Asset	Increases	Decreases
Liability	Decreases	Increases
Owners' Equity	Decreases	Increases
Revenue	Decreases	Increases
Expense	Increases	Decreases

In summary:

(1) Debits increase assets and decrease liabilities and owners' equity;

(2) Credits increase liabilities and owners' equity and decrease assets.

Rule 3. Debit is on the left and credit is on the right

There is at least one debit and one credit for each transaction. Usually, one of the accounts is a balance sheet account. Entries that are not made to a balance sheet account shall be made to the revenue accounts or expense accounts.

Notes

Double entry bookkeeping is a method of recording transactions, which allows a check on accuracy of the recording.

句中 which 引导的非限定性定语从句用来修饰 method。本句可以译为:
复式记账法是记录交易的一种方法，这种方法记账准确，便于核对。

2.4 Accounting Cycle

The accounting process is a series of activities that begins with a transaction and ends with the closing of the books. Because this process is repeated each reporting period, it is referred to as the accounting cycle.

Step 1

Transactions are analyzed on the basic of the business documents known as original vouchers and are recorded in recording vouchers.

Some types of original vouchers, such as a sales invoice, receipt, bill of lading, purchase order and so on, should be made for every transaction. Recording of transaction in a recording voucher is called making an entry. Each transaction recorded is a separate entry; it observes the rules of double-entry accounting and should be examined and approved strictly by certain persons.

原始凭证
记账凭证
销售发票
n. 收据/提货单/定购单

vt. 遵守

Step 2

Information is transferred from the recording vouchers to the subsidiary ledger accounts.

Each business transaction will be recorded in the account books scientifically, completely, and continuously, according to the accounting vouchers. This process is called posting. Debits and credits are transferred with the date of the vouchers recorded, as well as the summary which explains the source of the transaction in the vouchers, and the number of each voucher. Some specific types of frequently occured business transaction need to be recorded chronologically in an account book, called a journal. Some accounts, including cash and bank deposit account, are not only recorded in the subsidiary ledger, but also in the journal day by day.

n. 过账

adv. 序时地

Step 3

Prepare a trial balance from the account balance in the subsidiary ledger.

The equality of debits and credits posted to the ledger accounts can be verified by preparing a trial balance. A trial balance lists all the accounts in the order in which they appeared in the subsidiary ledgers with their current balances. If the computation of account balances has been accurate, the total of the accounts with debit balances must be equal to the total of the accounts with credit balances. A trial balance may be prepared at any time to test the equality of debits and credits in the ledgers.

账户余额

Step 4

Information is transferred from the subsidiary ledger accounts to the general ledger accounts.

The general ledger holds the individual accounts grouped according to the elements of financial statement. During this process, it often permits all entries to a given account to be added and posted as the aggregate amount.

Step 5

Adjusting entries are made to bring the balances of some accounts to their proper amounts for matching purposes.

It is often necessary to adjust some account balances at the end of each accounting period to achieve a proper matching of costs and expenses with revenue. These entries assign revenues to the periods in which they are earned, and expenses to the periods in which the related goods or services are used.

Step 6

Prepare financial statements.

Once the appropriate adjusting entries have been made and posted to the ledger accounts, an income statement and a balance sheet can he prepared directly from the account balances. In actual practice, however, many accountants find that drawing up a worksheet first will facilitate the preparation of the financial statements.

The worksheet is a columnar sheet of paper on which accountants have summarized information needed to make the adjusting entries and to prepare the financial statements. But it can never replace the financial statements or any entry in the accounts. When a worksheet is not used, financial statements are prepared directly from the data in the adjusted ledger accounts.

adj. 适当的

草拟
n. 工作底稿，工作表

adj. 分纵栏印刷或书写的

Step 7

Make closing entries.

The last step is closing procedure. Temporary or nominal accounts are maintained to facilitate the preparation of the income statement. Once the financial statements have been prepared for the current year, the balances of temporary accounts are closed or cleared by transferring their balances to another account called current year profits.

本年利润

Assignment

I. Select the best answer for each of the following questions or uncompleted sentences.

(1) Which of the following events is not an accounting transaction? _____.

    A. Purchasing an office building   B. Selling some inventories

    C. Paying income taxes   D. Hiring a payroll clerk

(2) The double-entry system requires that each transaction must be recorded _____.

    A. in at least two different accounts   B. in two sets of books

    C. in a journal and ledger   D. first as a revenue and then as an expense

(3) Owner invested cash in company: _____.

    A. increase cash account   B. decrease cash account

    C. both A and B are true   D. none of the above

(4) A credit is on the right-hand side of _____.

    A. an asset account only   B. a liability account only

    C. an owners' equity account only   D. all accounts

(5) Which of the following is a correct statement of the rules of debit and credit? _____.

    A. Debits increase assets and decrease liabilities

    B. Debits increase assets and increase owners' equity

    C. Credits decrease assets and decrease liabilities

    D. Credits increase assets and increase owners' equity

    E. None of the above

(6) Which of the following is not true? _____.

    A. Increases in assets are recorded as debits

    B. Increases in liabilities are recorded as debits

    C. Decreases in owners' equity are recorded as debits

    D. Increases in expenses are recorded as debits

    E. Increases in revenues are recorded as credits

(7) The left side of an account is referred to as _____.

    A. the balance   B. a debit

    C. a credit   D. a footing

(8) Which of the following debit and credit rules is correct? _____.

    A. Increases in owners' equity are recorded by credits

    B. Revenues are recorded by credits

    C. Decreases in owners' equity are recorded by debits

    D. Expenses are recorded by debits

    E. All of the above are correct

(9) A revenue account _____.
   A. is increased by debits
   B. is decreased by credits
   C. is increased by credits
   D. has a normal debit balance

(10) Adjusting entries are _____.
   A. not necessary if the accounting system is operating properly
   B. usually required before financial statements are prepared
   C. made whenever management desires to change an account balance
   D. made to balance sheet accounts only

II. Mark the correct items by "√" and the wrong items by "×".

(1) A business transaction produces only two effects on the accounting equation. (   )
(2) Revenues decrease owners' equity. (   )
(3) Whenever an expense is incurred, the owners' equity will be increased. (   )
(4) If the number of debit entries in an account is greater than the number of credit entries, the account will have a debit balance. (   )
(5) Debit means left, and credit means right. (   )
(6) A credit is an amount entered on the right-hand side of a ledger account. (   )
(7) Most companies have fewer asset account than liability accounts. (   )
(8) The owner invested cash in the company: increase capital account. (   )
(9) The business received cash from a credit client: decrease accounts receivable account. (   )
(10) The accounting cycle is the sequence of accounting procedures used to record, classify, and summarize accounting information. (   )

III. Case Analysis

May 1: Jill Jones and her family invested $8,000 in BHK Company and received 800 shares of stock.

May 2: BHK purchased a riding lawn mower for $2,500 cash.

May 8: BHK purchased a $15,000 truck. BHK paid $2,000 in cash and issued a note payable for the remaining $13,000.

May 18: BHK sold half of the repair parts to ABC Lawns for $150, a price equal to BHK cost. ABC Lawns agrees to pay BHK within 30 days.

May 29: BHK provided services for a client and received $750 in cash.

May 31: BHK purchased gasoline for the lawn mower and the truck for $50 cash.

Analyze the above transactions of BHK Company, set up its T-accounts, and prepare a trial balance.

Reading Material

Bookkeeping and Accounting

Accounting is often confused with bookkeeping. What is the difference between accounting and bookkeeping? Am I an accountant or a bookkeeper? Most people, even accountants, don't know the answer to these questions.

Well, in most cases the answer doesn't matter because bookkeeping and accounting share two basic goals: ①To keep track of your income and expenses, which improves your chances of making a profit; ②To collect the financial information necessary for filing your various tax returns. But, in other cases where someone wants to be technically correct the answer lies in what services a person performs.

Bookkeepers have always held vital positions in the companies they work for. They verify and balance receipts, post debits and credits, and record transactions. Some bookkeepers have offices in their own homes and make extra money in addition to their regular salary. In large companies, for instance, the bookkeeping cycle might be divided into departments such as Accounts Receivable, Accounts Payable, or Payroll. While these people are often referred to as "clerks", they might also be considered bookkeepers as they are "keeping the books" for a company. In small companies, the bookkeeper may perform the entire bookkeeping process, or might just enter data to give to the "accountant".

Thus, what is accounting? In brief, accounting includes bookkeeping but goes beyond it in scope. The accounting process is much less mechanical and more subjective. It begins with designing a system that will benefit the business, by capturing the financial information in a useful manner without being overly burdensome to the bookkeeper. Once the system is set up, the accountant analyzes and interprets financial information, prepares financial statements, conducts audits, makes forecasts and budgets, and provides tax services.

Since accounting requires an understanding of the bookkeeping process, accountants typically supervise the bookkeepers. Nowadays, for many businesses have much fewer employees, there is a good chance that the accountant will also be performing the bookkeeping role for a company.

Discussion questions:

(1) What is the difference between accounting and bookkeeping?
(2) What is the job of an accountant?

Unit 3

Current Assets

The simplification of anything is always sensation.

———G. K. Chesterton

Study Objectives

After studying this unit, you should be able to:
- Define current assets, cash, receivables and inventories.
- Identify the principles of cash control.
- Explain bank reconciliation.
- Identify the classification of receivables.
- Explain how discounts and bad debts are recognized in accounts.
- Describe the methods of determining inventory quantities.

Feature Story

People's Daily **Uncovers Defalcation of Poverty Relief Funds**

The central government gives some 25.3 billion yuan worth of poverty relief funds to local governments every year. In order to stamp out misuse of the funds, the ministry sets up a fund management system at the provincial level, and puts the funds directly into the accounts of local units that undertake poverty relief projects. *People's Daily* made public the names of local government departments and officials who were involved in the cases of defalcation of poverty relief funds. Among them, the former director of the office of poverty alleviation and development in Yunlian County of Sichuan Province, southwest China, defalcated with 1.7 million yuan of the relief funds in four years, accounting for nearly two-thirds of the total poverty relief funds that the central government had given to the county. The director misused the government money by building offices and apartment buildings, purchasing cars and other facilities, giving bonuses to the office staff, and paying for dinners and business trips. The ministry said in the news release that the offenders will be dealt with according to law and disciplined according to government rules. All the diverted funds will be retrieved.

These kinds of defalcation cases take place equally frequently in business circle where there exists imperfection in auditing and keeping accounts. As many corporation leaders take the advantage of the right to approve items for payment, improper diversions and uses of cash often occur in the name of reception fees and conference fees. Accordingly, close supervision of accounting and tight internal cash control are decisively vital, as cash could be easily concealed by anyone with a desire. In accountancy, cash is classified as an important quick current assets in a balance sheet.

In this unit, cash is first discussed, and then we will introduce other forms of current assets like receivables and inventories.

International Background Information

Current Assets

流动资产

Current assets are cash and other assets expected to be converted into cash, sold, or consumed either in one year or in the operating cycle, whichever is longer.[1] The operating cycle is the average time between the acquisition of materials and supplies and the realization of cash through sales of the products for which the materials and supplies were acquired. The cycle operates from cash through inventory, production, receivables, and back to cash. When there are several operating cycles within one year, the one-year period is used. If the operating cycle is longer than one year, the cycle period is used.

Current assets are presented in the balance sheet in order of liquidity (the ability to be converted to cash).[2] The five major items listed in the current assets section are cash, short-term investments, receivables, inventories, and prepayments.

Notes

1. Current assets are cash and other assets expected to be converted into cash, sold, or consumed either in one year or in the operating cycle, whichever is longer.
   流动资产是指现金和在一年内或超过一年的一个经营周期内变现、销售、或者耗用的资产。这里所谓的一年或者超过一年的一个经营周期内是指变现或者耗用的资产时间在一年内或者超过一年，但必须是在一个经营周期内。一个经营周期是指从外购、承担付款义务，到收回因销售商品或提供劳务而产生的应收账款的这段时间。
2. Current assets are presented in the balance sheet in order of liquidity (the ability to be converted to cash).
流动资产在资产负债表中按流动性强弱进行排列（流动性是指资产的变现能力）。

3.1 Cash

Assets are all the things which the firm owns or has title to. Firms may have current assets, fixed assets and other forms of assets. Current assets are cash and other items that can be converted into cash within a year or an operating cycle longer than that, such as cash, receivables, inventories, marketable securities, prepaid expenses, and short-term investment. A company's creditors will often be interested in how much that company has in current assets, since these assets can be easily liquidated in case the company goes bankrupt. In addition, current assets are important to most companies as a source of funds for day-to-day operations. The main current assets are cash, receivables and inventories.

被转换成……

n. 有价证券

n. 债权人
v. 清算
n. 破产

What Is Cash?

In general sense, cash refers to the notes and coins in the till and money on deposit in the bank. In accounting, cash means currency (coins, paper currency) on hand or on deposit in a bank or other depositories. Besides, those formal negotiable papers that will be due on demand are classified as cash for accounting purpose, including banker's drafts, cashier's checks, commercial drafts, certified checks and ordinary checks. Cash is the most active item on the accounting statements and is often called quick asset. It can be specified by the characteristics below:

• It's the asset that is readily transformed into any other type of asset, which makes it the most liquid asset owned by a company.

• Cash is easily concealed and transferred. It is the one asset most susceptible to improper distribution and use.

n. 钱柜

n. 储藏所/可兑取现金的票据/adj. 到期应支付的

速动资产/v. 具体说明
v. 转换，改变

v. 藏匿
adj. 易受影响的

Some companies use the term "Cash and Cash Equivalents" in reporting cash. Cash restricted for special purpose is reported separately as a current asset or as a non-current asset, depending on when the cash is expected to be used. If the restricted cash is expected to be used within the next year, it should be reported as current asset. Otherwise, it should be reported as long-term investment. Items such as postage stamps and postdated checks (checks payable in the future) are not cash. Stamps are reported as prepaid expense, and the postdated checks are accounts receivable.

Cash Control System

The basic contents of a cash control system are:

(1) To specify the range of cash payout.

Many of the business transactions of an entity are to be done by cash, such as:

• Payments of the employees' salaries, allowances, bonuses and fringe benefits.

• Allowances for business trip.

• Other petty payouts including postage, delivery services and small purchases of supplies.

International Insight

Among other potential restrictions, companies need to determine whether any of the cash accounts outside the country is restricted by regulations against exportation of currency.

(2) To control the amounts of cash on hand.

Companies find it both inconvenient and expensive to write checks for small expenditures, thus certain amounts of cash on hand may facilitate the daily petty expenses. The size of petty cash fund depends on an entity's actual situations. Many firms maintain funds that will last three or four weeks.

Because of the large volume and high frequency of cash transactions, numerous errors may occur in executing and recording them. To ensure the accuracy and reliability of the accounting records for cash, effective internal control over cash is necessary. The cash control system, which is part of a firm's internal control systems, has two main functions.

1. Internal Control over Cash Receipts

Cash inflows in most businesses come from numerous sources. The procedures used to attain adequate control may vary. However, the following procedures are important in all situations:

- Immediate counting of all cash received.
- Immediate recording of all cash received.
- Timely depositing of all cash received.

International Insight

Multinational corporations often have cash accounts in more than one currency. For financial statement purposes, these currencies are typically translated into U.S. dollars using the exchange rate in effect at the balance sheet date.

跨国公司

汇率
资产负债表日

Notes

Multinational corporations often have cash accounts in more than one currency. For financial statement purposes, these currencies are typically translated into U.S. dollars using the exchange rate in effect at the balance sheet date.
跨国公司通常有不止一种货币的现金账户。基于财务报告的目的，这些货币通常要在资产负债表日按汇率转化为美元。

2. Internal Control over Cash Disbursements

The cash outflows in most businesses are for a variety of reasons, such as to pay expenses and to purchase assets. Many cases of the cash defalcation occur in the disbursement process, because they are relatively easy to cover up unless there is an effective controlling system, such as:

- All cash disbursements are made by check with an exception of applying the petty cash system for small amount expenditures. Checks are signed, stored, written (and in some cases

n. 支出

n. 滥用

mailed) separately. Control is most effective when only one person is responsible for a given task. To achieve effective internal control over cash, establishment of responsibility and segregation of duties are the first step.

n. 划分

- Establish a petty cash system with tight control and close supervision.

n. 监控

- Prepare prenumbered checks and sign them only when approved invoices are provided.

- Supervise closely all cash-disbursement, related bookkeeping and periodic internal reports, and verify them periodically or aperiodically by a third independent party.

v. 核对

Bank Reconciliation

Generally, a business opens a checking account at the bank to facilitate transactions and to realize better control over cash. Cash inflows and outflows are, in most occasions, conducted through bank and daily cash receipts are deposited in bank, which minimizes the amounts of currency kept on hand. Additionally, the bank presents monthly bank statements to the company, showing a beginning cash balance, each performance of deposit and withdrawal within the month, and an ending cash balance of the company account. The company compares the bank statements with its internal cash records, then determines whether and why the errors or difference exists between them. All the errors and difference are recorded and adjusted in a bank reconciliation statement.

银行往来调节表，也称为银行存款余额调节表

n. 调和，调节

International Insight

A bank reconciliation is a schedule explaining any difference between the bank's and the company's records of cash. If the difference results only from the transactions not yet recorded by the bank, the company's record of cash is considered correct. But, if some part of the difference arises from other items, the bank's records or the company's records must be adjusted.

Reconciling items:

◇ Deposits in transit. End-of-month deposits of cash recorded

未达账项，在途存款

on the depositor's books in one month are received and recorded by the bank in the following month.

◇ **Outstanding checks.** Checks written by the depositor are recorded when written but may not be recorded (may not "clear") by the bank until the next month.   未兑现支票

◇ **Bank charges.** Charges are recorded by the bank against the depositor's balance for such items as bank services, printing checks, not-sufficient funds (NSF) checks, and safe-deposit box rentals. The depositor may not be aware of these charges until the receipt of the bank statements.   银行费用

◇ **Bank credits.** Collections or deposits by the bank for the benefit of the depositor may be unknown to the depositor until receipt of the bank statements. Examples are note collection for the depositor and interest earned on interest-bearing checking accounts.

◇ **Bank or depositor errors.** Errors on either the part of the bank or the part of the depositor cause the bank balance to disagree with the depositor's book balance.   错误

Two forms of bank reconciliation may be prepared. One form reconciles from the bank statement balance to the book balance or vice versa. The other form reconciles both the bank balance and the book balance to a correct cash balance. A sample of this form and its common reconciling items are shown as following:

Balance per Bank Statement (end of period)		$×× ×
Add: Deposits in Transit	$×× ×	
Undeposited Receipts (cash on hand)	$×× ×	
Bank Errors that Understate the Bank Statement Balance	$×× ×	$×× ×
Deduct: Outstanding Checks	$×× ×	$×× ×
Bank Errors that Overstate the Bank Statement Balance	$×× ×	$×× ×
Correct Cash Balance		$×× ×
Balance per Depositor's Book		$×× ×
Add: Bank Credits and Collections not yet Recorded in the Book	$×× ×	
Book Errors that Understate the Book Balance	$×× ×	$×× ×
		$×× ×
Deduct: Bank Charges not yet Recorded in the Book	$×× ×	
Book Errors that Overstate the Book Balance	$×× ×	$×× ×
Correct Cash Balance		$×× ×

This form of reconciliation consists of two sections: ① "balance per bank statement" and ② "balance per depositor's book." Both sections end with the same "correct cash balance". The correct cash balance is the amount to which the books must be adjusted and is the amount reported on the balance sheet. Adjusting journal entries are prepared for all the addition and deduction items appearing in the "balance per depositor's book" section. Any errors attributable to the bank should be called to the bank's attention immediately.

3.2 Receivables

Because a significant portion of sales and transactions are done without the immediate receipt of cash, companies must pay close attention to their receivables and manage them carefully. A business with many credit customers would set up the general ledger of accounts receivable and a separate account for each credit customer. The term "receivables" refers to amounts due from individuals and other companies (entities) within one year or the operating cycle, whichever is longer. Receivables generally include accounts receivable, notes receivable and non-trade receivables. Thereinafter, they are to be discussed and illustrated one after the other in the order they are listed on the balance sheet.

赊购客户

Accounts Receivable

Accounts receivable is defined as the kind of accounts used to record the claims on customers due from the sale of commodities and services, which are generally expected to be converted into cash in the regular course of business. Here in this unit, we focus on discounts and bad debts, which are two major elements in accounting for accounts receivable.

Discounts

Merchandisers and middlemen may offer discounts to purchasers, especially to wholesalers. Discounts are classified into

n. 中间商
n. 批发商

two types: trade discounts and cash discounts.

Trade discounts are the price reductions given by the seller mainly on the purpose of promoting its sales volume. The buyer pays for the goods and services at the invoice price (the list price minus a certain amount of discount). So the trade discounts are not recorded and cannot be shown in accounts.

If it be looked from the seller's angle, a cash discount is termed "sales discount" used either as a competitive measure to canvass for orders or as an incentive to encourage prompt payment.[1] In the sales agreement, it is usually expressed right after the price in two ways: for $××× per unit on terms of 1/10, n/eom; or for $××× per unit on terms of 3/10, n/50.[2] Cash discounts are to be recorded through the two alternative methods: gross method and net method.

By gross method, the accountants record the amounts of accounts receivable and sales at the invoice price. If the cash discount is taken ultimately by the buyer, a separate item named "sales discount" might appear to record the difference between the cash actually received and the amounts receivable. On the contrary, no cash discount is recorded. Net method is frequently used when the seller can be sure that the discount will be utilized just as the transaction is conducted. Thus the net sales amount (invoice price minus cash discount) is recorded both in accounts receivable and sales.

Bad Debts

When goods and services are sold on credit, there inevitably are some receivables that cannot be collected in due time for various reasons. The operating expenses or losses arising from the failure to collect receivables are so-called bad debts expenses or uncollectible accounts expenses. Such expenses or losses are considered a normal and necessary risk of doing business on a credit bases. Generally two methods below are used in accounting for uncollectible receivables.

1. Direct Write-off Method

Under the direct write-off method, a bad debt is recorded when a receivable is made certain to be uncollectible and the expense or loss is confirmed. The seller would then write off the account as an expense of the current accounting period. It is clear that in this way a bad debts expense is often recorded in a period different from the period in which the revenue was recorded. Consequently, with the use of this accounting method, both the income statement and the balance sheet may report the company's financial status less virtually and they cannot be regarded as forever-valid financial indexes for analytical purposes.

2. Allowance Method

With the drawbacks of the direct write-off method, many significant bad debts expenses are recorded in the allowance method, which involves estimating uncollectible accounts by periods. Under this method, an estimated uncollectible account is recorded at the end of each accounting period through an adjusting entry. Thus a better and more accurate matching between bad debts and income statement and balance statement is achieved.

Notes Receivable

Notes receivable represents claims supported by formal written promise issued by one party to another and are to be collected unconditionally within a specified time. Compared with accounts receivable, notes receivable are favored by the seller for the following merits:

• A note means a strong, legal claim to the maker or its endorsee.

• Notes can be converted into cash by discounting them to a bank at any time before the maturity date. And for this reason, the notes receivable account is listed above the accounts receivable account in the balance sheet.

• Interests may be earned with an interest-bearing note.

Non-Trade Receivables

Accounts and notes receivables arise from sales transactions of goods and services and are always considered to be the most important receivables possessed by a company. These two items together are called trade receivables. Non-trade receivables, judged from its name, are short-term receivables resulting either from the sale of non-merchandise assets or from other forms of claims not bearing upon any sales or transactions. Examples are loans to officers and company employees, interest and dividends receivable, and claims against insurance companies.

n. 股息，红利

Notes

1. If it be looked from the seller's angle, a cash discount is termed "sales discount" used either as a competitive measure to canvass for orders or as an incentive to encourage prompt payment.

   If 引导的从句中采用虚拟语气，省略了 should；词组 be termed 意为"被称作"。该句的意思是：

   现金折扣对卖方来说是一种销售折扣，是用来作为一种招揽订单的竞争手段，或作为一种鼓励即时付款的激励方式。

2. …for $×× × per unit on terms of 1/10, n/eom; or for $×× × per unit on terms of 3/10, n/50.

   1/10，n/eom 为专用条款，指买方若10日内支付，给1%折扣；10日以后1个月内支付则照发票价支付。

   3/10，n/50 为专用条款，指买方若10日内支付，给3%折扣；10日以后50日以内支付则按原价支付。

3.3 Inventories

Definition and Types of Inventories

Inventory is classified as a current asset and is used to refer to the merchandise and materials that will be converted into cash or consumed in the production within one year or during one operating cycle, whichever is longer. In our economy, inventories are an important barometer of business activity. The amount of inventories and the time required to sell or consume the goods at hand should be closely watched and indicated. Also a good balance must be maintained between too little inventory and too much. A company with too little inventory to meet demand will lose sales

n. 存货

n. 商品

n. 晴雨表

chances and slow down the production as well. One with too much inventory will be burdened with unnecessary carrying costs. In accounting, inventory affects the balance sheet, where it is frequently the most significant current asset. Inventory also affects the income sheet in the way of determining the production of operation for a particular period.

Merchandise inventory refers to the goods owned by the company and purchased for future sale in the ordinary course of business. For a manufacturer, inventories are not all for sale. A manufacturer's inventories include the followings:

- Raw material to be used in the production. 原材料
- Partially finished goods in process of manufacture. 半成品
- Finished goods ready for shipment to customers. 成品
- Low-valued and easily-damaged implements .

Inventory Systems

One of the two systems is used to account for inventory: a perpetual inventory system or a periodic inventory system. In the perpetual inventory system, detailed records of each inventory purchase and sale are maintained both in quantity and in value. This system continuously and dynamically shows the inventory that should be on hand for every item. However, the accuracy of the records must be tested by taking a physical inventory of each type of commodity at least once a year. The records are then compared with the actual quantities on hand and any differences are corrected.

永续盘存制/定期盘存制

adv. 动态地

实物盘存

Some businesses find it either unnecessary or uneconomical to invest in a computerized perpetual inventory system. Many small merchandising business managers still feel that a perpetual inventory system costs more than it worth. In a periodic inventory system, only the revenue from sales is recorded each time a sale is made. No entry is made at the time of the sale to record the cost of the merchandise that has been sold. Thus the cost of goods sold is determined only periodically by taking physical inventories at the end of the accounting period.

Inventory Measurement

In determining the cost of goods to be sold, two important phases are involved: determination of the quantities of the inventory items and determination of the unit cost of each inventory item. With regard to the calculation of the unit cost of the inventory, there are four frequently used methods.

(1) Last-in, First-out (LIFO)　　　　　　　　　　　　　后进先出法

The LIFO method assumes that the latest goods acquired are first to be sold, therefore, the unit cost of the latest goods purchased is to be assigned to unit cost of goods sold. This method is often used for goods in large quantity, such as sand, coal, etc.

(2) First-in, First-out (FIFO)　　　　　　　　　　　　　先进先出法

The FIFO method assumes that goods are used in the order in which they are purchased. In other words, it assumes that the first goods purchased are the first used or sold. The inventory remaining must therefore represent the most recent purchases.

(3) Average Cost Method (also called the weighed average cost method)　　　　　　　　　　　　　平均法　加权平均法

Under this method, goods sold and in inventory have the same cost per unit, and the average figure comes from the following formula:

Average Unit Cost = Total Cost of Goods/Total Units.

(4) Specific Identification Method　　　　　　　　　　　　　个别辨认法

This method is best used for inventories of high-valued such as cars and construction equipments. When the inventory is of a small unit price and involve large volumes, this method is not able to be carried out.

Assignment

Ⅰ. Select the best answer for each of the following questions or uncompleted sentences.

(1) The following are all cash except _____.

　　A. money orders　　B. coins　　C. stamps　　D. checks

(2) Internal control is used in a business to enhance the accuracy and reliability of its accounting records and to _____.

A. safeguard its assets　　　　B. prevent fraud

C. produce correct financial statements　　D. deter employee dishonesty

(3) **The statement that correctly describes the reporting of cash is that _____.**

A. cash cannot be combined with cash equivalents

B. restricted cash funds may be combined with cash

C. cash is listed first in the current assets section

D. restricted cash funds cannot be reported as current asset

(4) **T & D Company sells merchandise on Feb 15 on account to Punney Co. for $11,000, terms 2/10, n/30. On Feb 24, payment is received from Punney Co. for the balance due. The amount of cash received is _____.**

A. $11,000　　B. $10,780　　C. $11,220　　D. $220

(5) **Petty cash fund is _____.**

A. a cash fund used to pay for relatively small amounts

B. set aside by estimating the amount of cash needed for disbursements of relatively small amounts during a specified period

C. reimbursed when the amount of money in the fund is under the predetermined minimum amount

D. all of the above

(6) **Where should an investment in stock that is hold as a short-term investment be reported in the balance sheet? _____.**

A. Current assets　　　　B. Property, Plant and Equipment

C. Investments　　　　　D. None of the above

(7) **Which of the following is not the character of a manufacture's inventory? _____.**

A. It is owned by the company

B. It is kept for future sale

C. It belongs to current asset

D. It will be converted into cash or consumed in the production

(8) **Which of the following should not be included in the physical inventory of a company? _____.**

A. Goods held on consignment from another company

B. Goods shipped on consignment to another company

C. Goods in transit from another company shipped FOB shipping point

D. None of the above

(9) **In periods of rising prices, LIFO will produce _____.**

A. higher net income than FIFO

B. the same net income as FIFO

C. lower net income than FIFO

D. higher net income than average costing

(10) **In the perpetual inventory system, _____.**

A. LIFO cost of goods sold will be the same as in a periodic inventory system

B. average costs are based entirely on unit cost averages

C. a new average is computed under the average cost method after each sale

D. FIFO cost of goods sold will be the same as in a periodic inventory system

Ⅱ. Mark the correct items by "√" and the wrong items by "×".

(1) Current assets are cash and other assets expected to be converted into cash, sold, or consumed over one year. (   )

(2) Current assets are presented in the balance sheet in order of liquidity (the ability to be converted to cash). (   )

(3) The bank errors are not shown on the bank reconciliation. (   )

(4) It is not necessary to estimate the bad debts expense using the matching concept. (   )

(5) If prices are stable, the LIFO and weighted average cost method will report the same cost of goods sold and ending inventory. (   )

Ⅲ. Study the brief cases and fill in the blanks.

The following is the information about the oil inventory of Arlen Oil Company:

Beginning inventory (April 1st): 400 units; $1.00 per unit.

Purchase oil (April 10th): 300 units; $1.10 per unit.

Purchase oil (April 20th): 300 units; $1.20 per unit.

Ending inventory (April 30th): 600 units.

(1) The FIFO method assumes that the goods acquired first are first to be sold. Ending inventory is valued at the most recent purchase prices. Therefore, the ending oil inventory of Arlen Oil Company in April should be $_____.

(2) In LIFO method, it is assumed that the latest good acquired are first to be sold. So in the above case, the cost of oil sold in April should be $_____.

Ⅳ. Case Analysis

Hargrove Company has just completed its inventory count. It arrives at a total inventory of 200,000 units. You have been informed the information below:

(1) Goods held on consignment for Fred Co. of 15,000 units have been included in the inventory.

(2) Purchased goods of 10,000 units which are in transit (term: FOB shipping point) have not been included in the count.

(3) Sold inventory of 12,000 units which are in transit (term: FOB shipping point) have not been included in the count.

What should be the quantity of inventory of Hargrove Company?

Reading Material

What Is Money?

Everyone uses money. We all want it, work for it and think about it. However, the task of defining what money is, where it comes from and what it's worth seems to belong to the economists. While the creation and growth of money seems somewhat intangible, money is the way we get the things we need and want. Here we look at the multifaceted characteristics of money.

Medium of Exchange

Before the development of a medium of exchange—i.e., money—people would barter to obtain the goods and services they needed. This is basically how it worked: two individuals each having a commodity the other wanted or needed would enter into an agreement to trade their goods.

This early form of barter, however, does not provide the transferability and divisibility that makes trading efficient. For instance, if you have cows but need bananas, you must find someone who has not only bananas but also the desire for meat. What if you find someone who has the need for meat but no bananas and can only offer you apples? To get your meat, he or she must find someone who has bananas and wants apples... The lack of transferability of bartering for goods, as you can see, is tiring, confusing and inefficient. But that is not where the problems end: even if you find someone with whom to trade meat for bananas, you may not think a bunch of them is worth a whole cow. You would then have to find a way to divide your cow and determine how many bananas you are willing to take for certain parts of your cow.

To solve these problems came commodity money: a type of goods that functions as currency. In the 17th and early 18th centuries, for example, American colonialists used beaver pelts and dried corn in transactions. These kinds of commodities used for trade had certain characteristics: They were widely desired and therefore valuable, but they were also durable, portable and easily stored.

Another example of commodity money is gold. Unlike the beaver pelts and dried corn, gold is precious purely because people want it. It is not necessarily useful—after all, you can't eat it, and it won't keep you warm at night, but the majority of people think it is beautiful, and they know others think it is beautiful. So, gold is something you can safely believe has worth and it therefore serves as a physical token of wealth, based on people's perception.

If we think about this relationship between money and gold, we can gain some insight into how money gains its value—as a representation of something valuable.

Impressions Create Everything

The second type of money is fiat money, which does away with the need to represent a physical commodity and takes on its worth the same way gold did: by means of people's perception and faith. Fiat money was introduced because gold is a scarce resource and economies growing quickly couldn't always mine enough gold to back their money requirement. For a booming economy, the need for gold to give money value is extremely inefficient, especially when, as we already established, value is really created through people's perception. Fiat money then becomes the token of people's apprehension of worth—the basis for why money is created. An economy that is growing is apparently doing a good job of producing other things that are valuable to itself and to other economies. Generally, the stronger the economy, the stronger its money will be perceived and sought after. But, this perception, although abstract, must somehow be backed by how well the economy can produce concrete things and services that people want.

That is why simply printing new money will not create wealth for a country. Money is created by a kind of a perpetual interaction between concrete things, our intangible desire for them, and our abstract faith in what has value. Money is valuable because we want it, but we want it only because it can get us a desired product or service.

How Is Money Measured?

Sure, money is the $10 bill you lent to your friend the other day and don't expect back anytime soon. But exactly how much money is out there and what forms does it take? Economists and investors ask this question every day to see whether there is inflation or deflation. To make money more discernible for measurement purposes, they have separated it into three categories:

M1—This category of money includes all physical denominations of coins and currency, demand deposits, which are checking accounts and NOW (Negotiable Order of Withdrawal) accounts, and travelers' checks. This category of money is the narrowest of the three and can be better visualized as the money used to make payments.

M2—With broader criteria, this category adds all the money found in M1 to all time-related deposits, savings deposits, and non-institutional money-market funds. This category represents money that can be readily transferred into cash.

M3—The broadest class of money, M3 combines all money found in the M2 definition and adds to it all large time deposits, institutional money-market funds, short-term repurchase agreements, along with other larger liquid assets.

By adding these three categories together, we arrive at a country's money supply, or total amount of money within an economy.

Notes

barter	*n., v.* 换货，互换品，物物交换
beaver pelts	海狸毛皮
physical token	自然代币
fiat money	不兑现纸币
inflation	*n.* 通货膨胀，(物价) 暴涨
deflation	*n.* 通货紧缩，物价低廉（尤指成本不降低时的反常情形）
money supply	货币供应量

Discussion questions:

(1) Why is the early form of barter inefficient?

(2) What characteristics made beaver pelts and dried corn commodity money?

(3) Will a country be wealthier simply by printing more money? Why?

(4) Why is money valuable and desired by everyone?

(5) Give a definition of money by summarizing the features and functions of it.

Unit 4 Non-Current Assets

Study Objectives

After studying this unit, you should be able to:
- Determine the classification of non-current assets.
- Explain how to measure and report long-term investments in both common shares and bonds.
- Define and determine the costs of property, plant and equipment.
- Describe the two main methods of depreciation and how to apply them in accounting.
- Distinguish between revenue expenditures and capital expenditures during the useful life of property, plant and equipment.
- Indicate the scope of intangible assets.

Feature Story

Warren Buffett: How He Does It?

Did you know that a $10,000 investment in Berkshire Hathaway Inc. in 1965, the year Warren Buffett took control of it, would grow to be worth nearly $30 million by 2005? By comparison, $10,000 in the S&P 500 would have grown to only about $500,000. Whether you like him or not, Buffett's investment strategy is unquestionably the most successful ever since.

Here we look at how Buffett did it by asking himself some questions when he evaluates the relationship between a stock's level of excellence and its price. Keep in mind that these are not the only things he analyzes but rather a brief summary of what Buffett looks for:

1. Has the company consistently performed well?
2. Has the company avoided excess debt?
3. Are profit margins high? Are they increasing?
4. How long has the company been public?
5. Do the company's products rely on a commodity?

6. Is the stock selling at a 25% discount to its real value?

Buffett's investing style, like the shopping style of a bargain hunter, reflects a practical, down-to-earth attitude. The value-investing style is not perfect, perhaps. But whether you support Buffett or not, the proof is in the pudding. In 2018, he holds the title of the third-richest man in the world, with a net worth of $84 billion (Forbes 2018). Do note that the most difficult thing for any value investor, in our opinion anyways, including Buffett, is in accurately determining a company's intrinsic value.

In this unit, we'll introduce non-current assets, which include long-term investments, property/plant/equipment and intangible assets.

International Background Information

Non-Current Assets

Non-current assets are those not meeting the definition of current assets. They include a variety of items: long-term investments; property, plant and equipment; intangible assets; other assets.

非流动资产

缩写为PP&E，不动产、厂房和设备

Long-term investment, often referred to simply as investments, normally consists of four types:

长期投资

- ◇ Investments in securities, such as bonds, common stock, or long-term notes.

普通股
长期票据

- ◇ Investments in tangible fixed assets not currently used in operations, such as land held for speculation.
- ◇ Investments set aside in special funds such as a sinking fund, pensional fund, or plant expansion fund. The cash surrender value of life insurance is included here.
- ◇ Investments in non-consolidated subsidiaries or affiliated companies.

Property, plant and equipment are properties of a durable nature used in the regular operations of the company. These assets consist of physical property such as land, buildings, machinery, furniture, tools, and wasting resources (timberland, minerals). With the exception of land, most of these assets are either depreciable (such as buildings) or depletable (such an timberland or oil reserves).

n. 机器
n. 家具，设备

可耗减的

Intangible assets lack physical substance and are not financial instruments. They include patents, copyrights, franchises, goodwill, trademarks, and secret processes.

Other assets vary widely in practice. Some of the items commonly included are deferred charges (long-term prepaid expenses), non-current receivables, assets in special funds, deferred income taxes, property held for sale, and advances to subsidiaries.

递延资产, 递延费用/长期预付费/非流动应收账项

Notes

They include patents, copyrights, franchises, goodwill, trademarks, and secret processes.
无形资产包括专利、版权、特许经销权、商誉、商标和秘方。

4.1 Long-Term Investments

Long-term investments refer to the investments not intended to be realized within a year, including shares investment, bonds investment and other investments. A corporation invests in stocks of companies in a related industry or in an unrelated industry that the company wishes to enter to meet strategic goals such as gaining control of a competitor or moving into a new line of business.[1] In accordance with different situations, shares investment and other investments shall be accounted for by cost method or equity method respectively. This unit will discuss measuring and reporting long-term investments in both common shares (and stocks) and bonds.

股票投资
债券投资

成本法
权益法
普通股

Measuring and Reporting Investments in Common Shares

The accounting for an investment in common stock is based on the extent of the investor's influence over the operating and financial affairs of the investee.

An investor owning less than 20% of common stock of an investee would only exercise an insignificant influence over the investee, and in this situation the cost method of accounting is

n. 投资者
n. 被投资者

adj. 不重要的

used. Under this method, the investment is recorded at cost, and revenue is recognized only when dividends are received.

But when an investor owns between 20% and 50% of the common stock of a corporation, the equity method should be used, by which the investment is recorded at cost as under the cost method, but the investor records its share of the periodic net revenue of the investee and its cash or property dividends differently from under the cost method. An investor with a stock holding between 20% and 50% is presumed to have significant influence over the financial and operating activities of the investee. The investor may have a representative on the investee's board of directors. In this way the investor exercises some control over the investee.

A company that owns 50% and more of the common stock of another entity is known as the parent company. Because of its stock ownership, the parent company has a controlling interest in the subsidiary (affiliated) company. At this time, consolidated financial statements are usually prepared. These consolidated financial statements present the total assets and liabilities controlled by the parent company, and the total revenues and expenses of the subsidiary company as well.

Measuring and Reporting Investments in Bonds

Bonds investment must be accounted for according to actual amount paid. Where bonds are acquired at a premium or discount, the difference between the cost and the face value of the bonds shall be amortized over the periods prior to maturity of the bonds. Interest accrued during the period of bonds investment, and the difference between the amount of principal and interest received on bonds sold and their book cost and interest accrued but not yet received, shall be accounted for as current profit and loss.² Shares investment, bonds investment and other investments shall be shown separately in accounting statements at book balance.

Notes

1. A corporation invests in stocks of companies in a related industry or in an unrelated industry that the company wishes to enter to meet strategic goals such as gaining control of a competitor or moving into a new line of business.

   that the company wishes to enter 是用来修饰 an unrelated industry 的定语从句。

   to meet strategic goals such as gaining control of a competitor or moving into a new line of business 不定式用作目的状语。其中两个动名词 gaining…or moving…并列为 such as 的宾语，进一步解释说明 strategic goals。该句的意思是：

   企业购买同行或其他愿意涉足的行业的股份，是为实现一定的战略目标，如控制竞争对手或拓展新业务等。

2. Interest accrued during the period of bonds investment, and the difference between the amount of principal and interest received on bonds sold and their book cost and interest accrued but not yet received, shall be accounted for as current profit and loss.

   债券投资存续期内的应计利息，以及出售时收回的本息与债券账面成本及尚未收回应计利息的差额，应当计入当期损益。

4.2 Property, Plant and Equipment

Property, plant and equipment (fixed assets) include land (in China, land is treated as an intangible asset in accounting according to relevant laws), buildings and structures, machinery and equipment, transportation equipment, tools and implement, etc.

国际上习惯称为 Property, Plant and Equipment（不动产、厂房和设备），我国习惯称为 Fixed Assets（固定资产）

The features of property, plant and equipment can be summarized as follows:

• Long-lived and relatively permanent (the useful life is over one year generally).

adj. 持久的/使用年限

• Unit value is above the prescribed criteria.

规定的标准

• Original physical form remains unchanged during the process of utilization.

adj. 最初的，原始的

Acquisition Costs of Property, Plant and Equipment

At the acquisition date, property, plant and equipment are measured and recorded at cost in conformity with the cost principle. Cost consists of all expenditures that are necessary in acquiring the assets and making them ready for intended uses. The

与……一致

cost of land includes the cash purchase price plus other related closing costs, i. e. title and attorneys' fees, real estate brokers' commissions, and accrued property taxes. The cost of buildings consists of the contract price plus payment for the architects' fees, building permits and excavation costs. As for large equipment and implements, the cash purchase price and other related costs such as sales taxes, freight charges, and insurance during transit paid by the purchaser should be covered. As well, expenditures required in assembling, installing, testing, repairing and maintaining, renewing and improving the units should also be treated as part of the costs of the assets if the amounts are relatively large. And the small expenditures are treated as current operational expenses.

> **International Insight**
>
> Under international accounting standards, historical cost is the preferred treatment for property, plant and equipment. However it is also allowable to use revalued amounts. If revaluation is used, companies are required to revalue the classes of assets regularly.

Depreciation of Property, Plant and Equipment

After acquisition, measuring the expense of the asset during its useful life becomes necessary in accounting. All Property, plant and equipment except land should be charged to depreciation expense. Depreciation means a part of the value of the asset is gradually transferred to the cost of products or services because of wear and tear, or technological obsolescence during its useful life. Depreciation also means a process of cost allocation. Four factors should be taken into consideration when computing the depreciation of Property, plant and equipment:

• Cost—all expenditures that are necessary in acquiring an asset and making it ready for intended use.

• Useful Life—an estimate of its expected life, also called "service life", of an asset.

• **Salvage Value**—an estimate of its value at the end of its useful life.

• **Total Output**—an estimate of its working capacity (working hours of a machine, mileage of a truck, etc.).

Depreciation Method

1. Straight-Line Method

Under the Straight-line Method, the annual depreciation is the same for each year of the service life of an asset. In this sense, it is also called "Service-Life Method". This method sounds rational, and is more often applied when property, plant and equipment are used evenly in each accounting period. Assume that ABC Company bought a piece of plant asset at the cost of $15,000 with an estimated useful life of 4 years and an estimated salvage value of $800.

ABC Company Depreciation Schedule

Year	Depreciable Cost	Depreciable Rate	Annual Depreciation	Accumulated Depreciation	Book Value
1st yr	$14,200	25%	$3,550	$3,550	$11,450
2nd yr	$14,200	25%	$3,550	$7,100	$7,900
3rd yr	$14,200	25%	$3,550	$10,650	$4,350
4th yr	$14,200	25%	$3,550	$14,200	$800 (salvage value)

Note: Depreciable Cost = Cost − Salvage Value

Depreciable Rate = 100%/Useful Life

Annual Depreciation = Depreciable Cost × Depreciable Rate

Book Value = Cost − Accumulated Depreciation

2. Unit-of-Production Method

The Unit-of-Production Method relates depreciation to the use and the output asset rather than to the time of service life. Under this method, depreciation is determined by multiplying the output produced in the year by depreciation cost per unit. This method is especially used in some lines of business where the use frequency of certain property, plant and equipment varies greatly from period to period. In the above case, if the total output of the asset bought by ABC Company is 100,000 units (among which 5,000, 55,000, 35,000 and 5,000 units are of the first, second, third and fourth year respectively.), depreciation schedule under this method should then be as follows.

ABC Company Depreciation Schedule

Year	Depreciable Cost /Unit	Units of Output	Annual Depreciation	Accumulated Depreciation	Book Value
1st yr	$0.142	5,000	$710	$710	$14,290
2nd yr	$0.142	55,000	$7,810	$8,520	$6,480
3rd yr	$0.142	35,000	$4,970	$13,490	$1,510
4th yr	$0.142	5,000	$710	$14,200	$800
					(salvage value)

Note: Annual Depreciation = (Depreciable Cost/Unit) × Units of Output

There is another method known as Accelerated Depreciation Method, which includes Double-Declining Balance Method, Sum-of-Years'-Digits Method, Fixed-Percentage-on-Declining-Base-Amount Method, and Declining-Rate-on-Cost Method. Whatever method is applied, the objective is to select the one that best measures an asset's contributions to revenue over its useful life. Once a method is chosen, it should be used consistently all through the useful life of the asset.

加速折旧法
双倍余额递减法
年数总和法/固定比率折旧法/成本递减法

adv. 一贯地，始终如一地

International Insight

German companies depreciate their fixed assets at a much faster rate than U.S. companies because German tax laws permit accelerated depreciation of up to triple the straight-line rate.

Notes

German companies depreciate their fixed assets at a much faster rate than U. S. companies because German tax laws permit accelerated depreciation of up to triple the straight-line rate.
因为德国的税法允许加速折旧法的折旧率高达直线折旧法的三倍，所以德国公司固定资产的折旧速度比美国的要快很多。

Expenditures during the Useful Life

As stated above, expenditures of all kinds may happen during the useful life of a fixed asset. (property, plant or equipment)

1. Revenue Expenditures

A company may incur costs for ordinary repairs to maintain the operating efficiency, productive life and capacity of the unit. Examples are the oil addition of a motor, the replacing of the plumbing of the office building and worn-out gears on machinery. These frequently-occuring and fairy small amount of costs are recorded in revenue expenditures.

2. Capital Expenditures

Those infrequently-occuring and large amount of costs for additions and improvements for the purpose of increasing the operating efficiency and productive life and capacity of the unit are, on the contrary, referred to as capital expenditures.

Disposals of Property, Plant and Equipment

Property, plant and equipment may be disposed by the way of being retired, sold, or exchanged. At the time of disposal, it is necessary to determine the book value of the fixed assets. Whichever method of disposal is used, book value will be compared with the disposal result to get the "gain on disposal" or "loss on disposal". Both of the two items will be recorded in current income statement.

4.3 Intangible Assets

Definition and Characteristics of Intangible Assets

Intangible assets refer to the long-term assets that are of value because of the exclusive privileges and rights to their owners and have no physical existence, including patents, copyrights, trademarks and trade names, franchises, etc. Several important characteristics are included in the definition of intangible assets.

（1） **No Physical Existence**

This is the chief characteristic and main evidence in identifying an intangible asset. By this characteristic, intangible assets are distinguished from fixed assets.

（2） **For Long-Term Service**

An intangible asset is expected to bring benefit in more than one operating period for an entity. This characteristic makes intangible assets different from current assets, and they are classified as non-current assets.

（3） **Monopolistic**

An intangible asset is an exclusive right often monopolized by a single entity. The monopoly over intangible assets is protected against being shared by laws or other government regulations.

（4） **Uncertainty of the Revenue**

It is very difficult to predict the amount of the revenue arising from an intangible asset. In addition, the revenue brought by a certain intangible asset is also difficult to be distinguished from the revenue brought by other assets. Consequently, there is hardly a way to recognize the corresponding amount of revenue respectively.

Intangible assets obtained through purchase shall be accounted for at actual cost. Intangible assets received from investors shall be accounted for at the assessed value or the amount specified in the contract. Self-developed intangible assets shall be accounted for at actual costs in the development process. All intangible assets shall be averaged and amortized periodically over the period benefited from such expenditures and be shown with unamortized balance on the accounting statement.

Patents

A patent is an official right granted by the relevant government institution (the State Intellectual Property Office), enabling its owner exclusive rights to the patented device for 20 years.

Copyrights

An official right granted by the government institution, giving its owner exclusive right to publish, reproduce and sell his writings or other forms of artistic works for a period of not more than 50 years beyond the author's death, is called a copyright.

n. 版权

Trademarks and Trade Names

A trademark or a trade name is a word, phrase, or symbol that identifies a particular enterprise or product. Examples are "Lenovo", "Coca-Cola", the letter "M" for "McDonald's" and such like. Trademarks and trade names play a great role in determining the sales volumes and popularity of the enterprises and their products.

n. 商标

在……方面起重要作用
销售量

Franchises

A franchise is a right granted to an organization or an individual by the government or a company to conduct specific business in a designated geographical area. Licenses to use city streets to operate a bus line, as well as the rights to sell certain products in a certain district, are examples of this.

n. 特许权

adj. 指定的

Notes

Intangible assets refer to the long-term assets that are of value because of the exclusive privileges and rights to their owners and have no physical existence, including patents, copyrights, trademarks and trade names, franchises, etc.

无形资产是指那些没有实物形态的长期资产，这类资产因其所有者独占某种权利和特权而有价值，包括专利权、著作权、商标和商号权、特许权等。

Assignment

Ⅰ. Select the best answer for each of the following questions or uncompleted sentences.

(1) The equity method of accounting for long-term investments in stock should be used when the investor owns _____.

    A. less than 20% of the common stock of the investee

    B. more than 20% of the common stock of the investee

    C. between 20% and 50% of the common stock of the investee

    D. more than 50% of the common stock of another entity

(2) The parent company has _____ on the subsidiary.

A. controlling influence B. significant influence
C. insignificant influence D. no influence

(3) **Which of the following is not a type of long-term investments?** _____.

A. Stocks, bonds and similar securities of another company held on a long-term basis

B. Loans to affiliates or subsidiaries

C. Investments in low-risk, high-liquidity, short-term securities such as government-issued securities

D. Cash value of life insurance on company executives

(4) **Which of the following is not a characteristic of property, plant and equipment?** _____.

A. Tangible B. Long-lived
C. Unchanged outlook D. For resale

(5) **In accounting, which of the following factors is not an estimate to determine the depreciation of a fixed asset?** _____.

A. Cost B. Useful life
C. Salvage value D. Total units of output

(6) **If the market rate of interest is lower than the stated rate, bonds will be sold at an amount** _____.

A. equal to face value

B. not determinable from the given information

C. lower than face value

D. higher than face value

(7) **Which of the following items is depreciated?** _____.

A. Land B. Inventory
C. Equipment D. Cash

(8) **A company can minimize its net income in the first year of owning an asset, if it uses the** _____.

A. straight-line method

B. unit-of-production method

C. sum-of-the-years'-digits method

D. double-declining-balance method

(9) **Which type of account should accumulated depreciation be?** _____.

A. An asset account.

B. A liability account

C. An owners' equity account

D. A temporary account

(10) All of the followings are intangible assets except _____.

    A. patents   B. loan to debtors

    C. goodwill   D. franchises

Ⅱ. Study the brief cases and fill in the blanks.

(1) The cost of a fixed asset consists of all expenditures that are necessary in acquiring the asset and making it ready for its intended use. Among them the costs for transportation and installation are involved. Assume that Plymouth Bank buy a computer for $18,000 and pay $200 for transportation fee plus $100 for installation fee. The cost of the equipment should be reported as $_____.

(2) An oven is bought at $30,000 with an estimated service life of 14 years and salvage value of $2,000. In this case, the depreciation cost should be: ① $_____. Under the Straight-Line Method, the depreciation value for each year is: ② $_____.

(3) When using the Unit-of-Production Method, depreciation is determined by multiplying the units of output produced in the year by depreciation per unit. Assume that Grandy Company bought a track at $44,000 in 2017. The track was expected to travel 100,000 miles, and its salvage value would be $4,000.

Its depreciation cost: ① $_____.

The estimated cost per mile: ② $_____.

In 2018, the track traveled 15,000 miles. The depreciation value in 2018 is ③ $_____.

(4) A fixed asset is with a cost of $40,000, and its accumulated depreciation is $30,000. It is sold at $12,000. An entry as follows should be made at disposal:

Cash	$12,000
Accumulated Depreciation	① $_____
Property, plant and Equipment	② $_____
Gains on Disposal	③ $_____

Ⅲ. Case Analysis

A farming entity bought a plane for $22,000, plus sales tax of $1,300 and delivery cost of $600. The company paid $200 for painting, $1,000 for refitting, $800 for an annual insurance policy, and $90 for a plane license. Useful life: 10 years. Estimated working capacity: 10,000,000 acres.

    ① Determine the cost of this fixed asset.

    ② Determine the depreciation for each of the first two years by the Straight-line Method.

    ③ Determine the depreciation for each of the first two years by the Unit-of-production Method.

       (The first year: 19,000 acres. The second year: 2,500,000 acres.)

Reading Material

Pros and Cons of Leasing vs. Buying a Vehicle

Buying a car can be overwhelming. In fact, the pleasure of getting a new car can be quickly clouded during the financing decision-making process and price negotiations. Besides price negotiations, many car shoppers are faced with the decision to lease or buy. Which financing decision is right and why? This article will focus on the two choices.

Trends

As new cars become more and more expensive, more buyers will likely be forced to lease. In fact, some auto experts predict that within twenty years, everyone will be leasing their cars. A car payment may become a fixed budgetary expense, much like your mortgage.

For those of us who have never leased a car, this statement may be disturbing. Leases seem confusing, complicated and geared more toward business owners (who might deduct the expense) or individuals who simply can't afford car payments. But these may be outdated. Before considering the two financing options, car-buyers need a solid understanding of the different purchasing processes.

Buying: the Benefits

By far the greatest benefit of buying a car is that you may actually own it one day. What implied in this benefit is that you'll one day be free of car payments. The car is yours to sell at any time and you are not locked into any type of fixed ownership period.

When you buy a car, the insurance limits on your policy are typically lower than if you leased. Finally, by owning a car, you're free while driving without penalties or restrictions.

Buying: the Drawbacks

The most obvious downside of owning versus leasing is the monthly payment, which is usually higher on a purchased car. Additionally, the dealers usually require a reasonable down payment, so the initial out-of-pocket cost is higher when buying a car.

Presumably, as you pay down your car loan, you have the ability to build equity in the vehicle. Unfortunately, however, this is not always the case. When you purchase a car, your payments reflect the whole cost of the car, usually amortized over a four-to-six-year period. But depreciation can take a nasty toll on the value of your car, especially in the first couple of years you own it. More and more, as car prices escalate, buyers who give modest down payments end up financing a considerable portion of the cars, and then find themselves in an "upside-down situation" where the car is worth less than what the buyer pays to own it.

Like the monthly payments of a mortgage, monthly car payments are divided between paying principal and interest, and the amounts dedicated to each vary from payment to payment. In the first year in which you pay back your car loan, the majority of each payment goes towards interest rather than principal. But in the first couple years after being purchased, most new vehicles depreciate

20%-40%. The loss in equity may be doubled: your car depreciates dramatically, and the monthly payments you've been making have mostly gone towards interest rather than the principal, which leaves you very little equity in the car.

Leasing: the Benefits

Perhaps the greatest benefit of leasing a car is the lower out-of-pocket costs of acquiring and maintaining the car. Leases require little or no down payment and there are no up-front sales tax payments. Additionally, monthly payments are usually lower, and you get the pleasure of owning a new car every few years.

With a lease, you are essentially renting the car for a fixed number of months (typically 36-48 months). Therefore, you pay only for the use (depreciation) of the car for that period, and you are not forced to absorb its full depreciation cost. Leasing a car will never put you in an upside-down position.

Leasing also provides an alternative when buying a car is not an option. Most banks will not lend more than $30,000 for a car loan. If you are planning to acquire a car worth more than that, leasing may be your only option.

Finally, for business owners, leasing a car may offer tax advantages if the vehicle is used for business purposes.

Leasing: the Drawbacks

By leasing a car, you always have a car payment, and if you don't like that, then leasing is probably not right for you. As long as you lease, you never really own it. However, when your lease term is up, it depends on your type of lease. You either hand the keys over to the car dealership and look for another vehicle, or finance the remaining value of the vehicle and go from making lease payments to loan payments.

The mileage restrictions of leasing is regarded as another drawback. If you drive a great deal during the year, consider a loan or an open-end lease instead. Most leases restrict your mileage usage to 15,000 miles per year (sometimes even lower at 12,000 per year). If you go over your allotted miles, you pay the extra: the going rate is about 15 cents for every mile over your limit, and 20-25 cents for luxury cars. So, if you go over 4,000 miles on your luxury sedan, you can expect to pay about $800 at the end of the lease.

Finally, insurers usually require higher coverage costs for leased vehicles. However, depending on your age, driving record and place of residence, that additional cost may be nominal.

Conclusion

The decision to lease or buy will always depend on your personal circumstances. If your objective is one day to be rid of car payments and you actually want to take ownership, buying a car may be the best option. If, however, your goal is to drive a new set of wheels every few years and minimize your monthly costs, leasing a car may be a good alternative.

Acquainting yourself with the two financing options will give you the confidence you need when stepping into a dealer's showroom.

Notes

lease	*v.* 租赁
mortgage	*n.* （尤指购房时的）抵押贷款
down payment	首期付款

Exercises:

Decide whether the statements are True (T) or False (F) according to the passage:

(1) When you buy a car, you may enjoy the benefits of having lower insurance limits and suffer from the drawback of being not able to build equity in the vehicle. (   )

(2) If you choose to buy your car on amortization, you have to consider the factors such as the down payment, the monthly payments, but not depreciation. (   )

(3) By leasing, you will have no tax obligations, no mileage restrictions, lower monthly payments and lower or even no down payment. (   )

(4) When your lease term becomes due, the lessee may choose to pay off the remaining value of the vehicle and go from making lease payments to loan payments. (   )

(5) It can be inferred that the writer of this article is inclined to lease a car. (   )

Unit 5

Liabilities

Study Objectives

After studying this unit, you should be able to:
- Define liabilities, current liabilities and long-term liabilities.
- Identify the major types of current liabilities and long-term liabilities.
- Explain current ratio and its implication.
- Describe the features of different types of bonds.
- Determine on what conditions bonds are sold at discount or at premium.
- Explain debt to total asset ratio, times interest earned ratio and their implications.

Feature Story

Macro is an old brand and has a good reputation in the business of gas stove appliances. Like every business, it was faced with fierce competition from the very beginning. For the years, Macro has put great effort in distribution channels expanding and products researching and developing. Despite all these exertions, it is still far from gaining a favorable internal operating surrounding and achieving the company's strategic goal. In 2004, its current liabilities amounted to ￥258.05 billion, and short-term credit amounted to ￥102 billion, which made its debt to total asset ratio up to 81.41%. Consequently, Macro was burdened with an interest expense totalling ￥106.52 million.

In May of 2005, Macro declared that it would transfer 90% shares of XieKai Real Estate Co., Ltd. In expectation to trade out its land resources to reduce bank debts, Macro proclaimed to gather its energy and forces to concentrate on its main business lines: gas stove appliances and transformer. The case of Macro reveals to us some special terms like "debt to total asset ratio", liabilities, current liabilities and so on. Hereinafter we are to discuss more about liabilities.

International Background Information

What Is a Liability?

The question, "what is a liability?" is not easy to answer. For example, one might ask whether preferred stock is a liability or an ownership claim. The first reaction is to say that preferred stock[1] is in fact an ownership claim and should be reported as part of stockholders' equity. In fact, preferred stock has many elements of debt as well. The issuer (and in some cases the holder) often has the right to call the stock within a specific period of time—making it similar to a repayment of principal. The dividend is in many cases almost guaranteed (cumulative provision)—making it look like interest. And preferred stock is but one of many financial instruments that are difficult to classify.

To help resolve some of these controversies, the FASB defined liabilities as "probable future sacrifice of economic benefits arising from present obligations of a particular entity to transfer assets or provide services to other entities in the future as a result of past transactions or events".[2]

In other words, a liability has three essential characteristics:
◇ It is a present obligation that entails settlement by probable future transfer or use of cash, goods or services.
◇ It is an unavoidable obligation.
◇ The transaction or other event creating the obligation has already occurred.[3]

Because liabilities involve future disbursements of assets or services, one of their most important features is the date on which they are payable. Currently maturing obligations must be satisfied promptly and in the ordinary course of business if operations are to be continued. Liabilities with a more distant due date do not, as a rule, represent a claim on the enterprise's current resources and are therefore in a slightly different category. This feature gives rise to the basic division of liabilities into two parts: current liabilities and long-term liabilities.

n. 权利
n. 本金 / *n.* 股息，股利

n. 利息

到期日，支付日

Notes

1. preferred stock 优先股

   优先股是相对于普通股而言的，主要指在利润分红及剩余财产分配的权利方面，优先于普通股。

   优先股的主要特征：①优先股通常预先定明股息收益率。由于优先股股息率事先固定，因此优先股的股息一般不会根据公司经营情况而增减，而且一般也不能参与公司的分红，但优先股可以先于普通股获得股息，对公司来说，由于股息固定，它不影响公司的利润分配。②优先股的权利范围小。优先股股东一般没有选举权和被选举权，对股份公司的重大经营无投票权，但在某些情况下可以享有投票权。③如果公司股东大会需要讨论与优先股有关的索偿权，则优先股的索偿权先于普通股，而次于债权人。

2. …the FASB defined liabilities as "probable future sacrifice of economic benefits arising from present obligations of a particular entity to transfer assets or provide services to other entities in the future as a result of past transactions or events".

   美国财务会计准则委员会（FASB）把负债定义为"由于过去的交易或事项所引起的某一特定主体的现有债务，这种债务需要企业在将来以转移资产或提供劳务加以清偿，从而引起未来经济利益的流出"。

3. … a liability has three essential characteristics:

   ◇ It is a present obligation that entails settlement by probable future transfer or use of cash, goods or services.

   ◇ It is an unavoidable obligation.

   ◇ The transaction or other event creating the obligation has already occurred.

   负债有三个基本特征：①负债是现时的义务，需要在将来以现金、商品或服务来偿还；②负债是一种不可回避的义务；③导致负债产生的交易或其他事项已经发生。

5.1 Current Liabilities

Definition and Classification of Current Liabilities

Liabilities are debts borne by an enterprise, measurable by money value, which will be paid to a creditor by using assets or services. Liabilities are generally classified into current liabilities and long-term liabilities.

Current liabilities refer to the obligations that are reasonably expected to be paid on demand from existing current assets or through the creation of other current liabilities. As in the case of current assets, the time period for payment of a current liability is no more than one year or one operating cycle, whichever is lon-

n. 债务

ger. Current liabilities include:

(1) **Notes and Accounts Payable**

Notes payable and accounts payable due within one year are accounted as current liabilities. Whenever bank loans are obtained, notes payable are issued. Notes payable are also issued on other occasions including the purchase of a real estate or costly equipment, and sometimes other kinds of purchasing. Notes maybe classified as short-term or long-term, depending upon the payment due date. Notes may also be interest-bearing or non-interest-bearing.

Accounts payable are short-term debts to suppliers for the purchase of goods or acquisition of services. The period of such extended credit is usually found in the terms of the sale (e. g. , 2/10, n/30) and is commonly 30 to 60 days.

(2) **Accrued Expenses**

Accrued expenses include rentals payable, taxes payable, interests payable, and stuff and workers salaries, bonus and welfare funds.

应计费用
n. 租金
n. 奖金
n. 福利

(3) **Unearned Revenues**

Unearned revenues are money received before goods are delivered or services are rendered.

v. 提供

International Insight

In USA, how do the companies account for unearned revenues that are received before goods are delivered or services are rendered?

1) When the advance is received, the cash account is debited, and a current liability account identifying the source of the unearned revenues is credited.

2) When the revenues are earned, the unearned revenues account is debited, and an earned revenues account is credited.

(4) **Current Maturity of Long-Term Debts**

Long-term liabilities to be matured and payable within a year shall be shown as a separate item under current liabilities.

(5) **Contingent Liabilities**

Obligations and their value are not yet determined, and are

或有负债

still dependent or contingent upon some future events. A contingent liability will either develop into a real liability, or be eliminated entirely by a future event. Examples are income tax, the liability for future warranty repairs on goods sold, etc.

Current liabilities can be classified on whether the amount is definite. In this way, there are current liabilities of definite value, estimated liabilities and contingent liabilities. Current liabilities are generally listed on the balance sheet either according to the date from the earliest to the latest, or in the order of the value from the largest to the smallest.

adj. 因（情况）而变的，看……而定的

> **International Insight**
>
> In Switzerland, companies may make provisions for general (non-specified) contingencies to the extent allowed by tax regulations.

Current Ratio

Users of financial statements look closely at the relationship between current assets and current liabilities. This relationship is important in evaluating a company's liquidity—its ability to pay short-term debts. When current assets exceed current liabilities at the balance sheet date, the likelihood for paying the liabilities is favorable. When the reverse is true, short-term obligations may not be able to be paid, and the company may ultimately be forced into bankruptcy. Current ratio is current assets divided by current liabilities. Current ratio makes it possible for the users to compare the liquidity of different companies or of the same company at different times. Higher ratio stands for healthier internal operating surroundings and better external credit ranking of the company. An investor, for example, will consider and compare carefully the current ratio of many companies where he or she wants to invest his money before making a final decision. Similarly, suppliers and banks will not neglect this ratio before selling goods on account or crediting a loan to the customer. Even employees want it to evaluate whether their choice to work in the company is sound for fear of nonpayment. This ratio is the essential information for the external users of financial statements in supporting their decisions or judgments.

n. 流动性，偿债能力

n. 相反，反面

流动比率

Notes

Higher ratio stands for healthier internal operating surroundings and better external credit ranking of the company.

词组 stand for 是"代表、表示"的意思。该句的意思是:

流动比率越高,表示公司内部运作环境越健全,公司外部信用地位越好。

5.2 Long-Term Liabilities

Long-term liabilities are company's obligations that extend beyond the current year or alternatively beyond the current operating cycle, including long-term loans payable, bonds payable, long-term accounts payable, etc. Besides, deferred income taxes, endowment insurance for the employees, liability for severance pay, liability for vacation pay are also included in long-term liabilities.

递延所得税
养老保险/解雇费,员工安置费

Long-Term Loans Payable

Long-term loans payable include the loans borrowed from financial institutions and other units. It shall be accounted independently according to the different characters of the loan and at the amount actually incurred.

Long-Term Accounts Payable

Long-term accounts payable include accounts payable for importing equipment, accounts payable for fixed assets financed by leasing. Long-term accounts payable shall be accounted at actual amounts.

The two most common types of leases are operating leases and capital leases. In an operating lease, the lessor continues to own the property and the lessee just uses the property temporarily. So the rental payments are recorded as an expense in the income statement. But, in some cases, the lease contract transfers all the benefits and risks of ownership to the lessee. Such a lease is actually a purchase of the property. This type of lease is called a capital lease. A capital lease, although legally a rental

经营租赁
融资租赁/n. 出租方
n. 承租方

case, is in substance an installment purchase by the lessee. A lease is recognized as a capital lease if any one of the following conditions exists:

- During the lease term, the lessee can purchase the asset at a lower price than its market value at his option, the ownership of the asset is transferred to the lessee.
- The lease term is equal to 75% or more of the useful life of the asset.
- The total amount of rental payments during the lease term is equal to or more than 90% of the market value of the asset.

In the above conditions, the leased asset is reported in the balance sheet under fixed assets. The part of liability expected to be paid in the next year is reported as a current liability, while the remainder is classified into a long-term liability. Recently capital lease has been a wide-spread way of collecting funds, which is favored by the domestic companies and companies abroad. Compared with buying a fixed asset by creating long-term loans, capital lease is more convenient, and the cost can be paid back earlier, thus it is a better alternative.

Bonds Payable

The above two forms of financing involve finding an individual, a company, or a financial institution willing to supply the needed funds. Bonds, however, are issued to obtain large amount of long-term capital. Bonds have many different kinds, and each has its particular feature. Some bonds can be converted into common stock at the bondholder's option, known as convertible bonds. Others that are subject to redemption at a stated amount prior to maturity at the option of the issuer, are called callable bonds. Furthermore, there are secured bonds and unsecured bonds depending on whether bonds have specific assets pledged as collateral; term bonds and serial bonds depending on whether maturing at a specified date or maturing in installments; registered bonds and bearer bonds depending on whether they are issued in the name of owner.

市场价格/n. 选择

n. 剩余部分

adj. 国内的

可转换债券

可提前（可通知）赎回债券/担保债券/无担保债券

n. 抵押品/定期债券/分期还本债券/n. 分期付款/记名债券/不记名债券

Whatever kind, bonds are a form of interest-bearing notes payable.

If the contractual interest rate (often called nominal interest rate) equals the market interest rate (called effective interest rate) by coincidence, bonds are sold at face value. However, this seldom happens because market interest rates change daily, which makes it hardly possible for a company to estimate the exact market interest rate of selling bonds when printing the bond certificates. As a result, bonds are more often sold at an amount different from face value. They are sold at a discount if the contractual interest rate is lower and sold at a premium in case the market interest rate is lower. The amortization of bonds premiums and discounts should be recorded and reported separately in each accounting period in either Straight-line Method or Effective Interest Method. Accordingly, the sale of bonds at a discount does not represent the issuer's bad financial situation, nor does the sale of bonds at premium mean outstanding financial strength.[1] Long-term creditors are particularly interested in a company's ability to pay due interest and the ability to pay back the face value at maturity. The following two ratios can be of some referential value for the investors:

(1) **Debt to Total Asset Ratio**

It is calculated by dividing total liabilities (current and long-term) by total assets. Higher debt to total asset ratio indicates the greater possibility that the company fails to pay out the bonds at due time.

(2) **Times Interest Earned Ratio**

This ratio computed by dividing income before income taxes and interest expense by interest expense, implies the company's ability to pay interests as they come due or the extent of which earnings are available to meet interest payments.[2] A lower times interest earned ratio means that less earnings are available to meet interest payments and the business is less possible to increase the interest rates.

息票利率/名义利率
市场利率/实际利率
巧合地/票面价值

直线摊销法
实际利率法

资产负债比

已获利息倍数

International Insight

Valuation of long-term debts varies internationally. In the U.S., discount and premium are booked and amortized over the life of the debt. In some countries (e.g., Sweden, Japan, Belgium), it is permissible to write off the discount and premium immediately.³

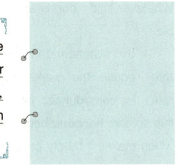

Notes

1. Accordingly, the sale of bonds at a discount does not represent the issuer's bad financial situation, nor does the sale of bonds at premium mean outstanding financial strength.

   nor 常用作连词,用于有 neither、not 或其他表否定意义的上下文中,意为"也不"。上句因 nor 放在句首引起句子倒装。例如:My brother doesn't like it, nor do I.

   上句的意思是:

   因而债券折价销售并不代表发行者财务状况令人担忧,债券溢价销售也不能说就意味着其财务实力雄厚。

2. This ratio, computed by dividing income before income taxes and interest expense by interest expense, implies the company's ability to pay interests as they come due or the extent of which earnings are available to meet interest payments.

   as they come due 中的 they 指代 interests。该句的意思是:

   已获利息倍数通过息税前利润(即未扣除所得税和利息费用的利润)除以利息费用而计算得出,它表示公司支付到期利息的能力或用所得来支付利息的程度。

3. Valuation of long-term debts varies internationally. In the U.S., discount and premium are booked and amortized over the life of the debt. In some countries (e.g., Sweden, Japan, Belgium), it is permissible to write off the discount and premium immediately.

   各国对长期负债的估价各不相同。在美国,对折价和溢价部分要在负债期内进行记录和摊销。而在另一些国家,如瑞典、日本、比利时,是允许对折价和溢价部分进行直接转销的。

Assignment

Ⅰ. Select the best answer for each of the following questions or uncompleted sentences.

(1) The time period for classifying a liability as current is one year or the operating cycle, whichever is _____.

   A. longer   B. shorter

   C. probable   D. possible

(2) To be classified as a current liability, a debt must be expected to be paid _____.

    A. out of existing current assets

    B. by creating other current liabilities

    C. within 2 years

    D. both A and B

(3) **Current ratio is calculated as** _____.

    A. current assets/current liabilities

    B. current liabilities/current assets

    C. current assets – current liabilities/current liabilities

    D. current liabilities – current assets/current assets

(4) Golden Shirley Company borrows $108,000 on September 1, 2013 from Ohio State Bank by signing a $108,000, 11% payable semiannually, one-year note. What is the accrued interest at December 31, 2006? _____.

    A. $11,880   B. $3,960

    C. $108,000   D. $5,940

(5) The term used for bonds that are issued in the name of the owner is _____.

    A. bearer bonds   B. registered bonds

    C. secured bonds   D. callable bonds

II. Mark the correct items by "√" and the wrong items by " × ".

(1) Current liabilities are those obligations that will normally be paid within the next year. (　　)

(2) Current liabilities are one of two kinds: known amounts or estimated amounts. (　　)

(3) Liabilities are what the business is due from its customers. (　　)

(4) It is a fact that in practice, bond premiums, having or reflecting superior quality or value, are rare because few companies issue their bonds to pay cash interest above the market interest rate. (　　)

(5) Current portion of long-term debt is presented in current liabilities section on the balance sheet. (　　)

III. Study the brief cases and finish the exercises.

1. Assume that Green Company raises cash $100,000 from the bonds issued with a face value of $100,000. Please record the transaction in the accounting entries of "Cash" and "Bonds payable".

    Dr. _____   _____

    Cr. _____   _____

2. When issuing bonds, an entity is to be burdened two obligations: One is to pay back the face value at maturity, which is the principle of the bonds; the other is to pay the interest semiannually. The liabilities to pay back the principal are usually classified into (current/non-current) liabil-

ities; the unpaid interests are often called (current/non-current) liabilities.
3. In the balance sheet of Garsden Company, current liabilities such as the accounts payable are regarded as a request upon (current assets/all assets) of the company.
4. A contingent liability should be recorded in the accounts when:
   i. It is (probable/definite) that the contingency will happen.
   ii. The amount (can/cannot) be reasonably estimated.
5. Jeffery earns $14 per hour for a 40-hour week and $21 per hour for any overtime work. If Jeffery woks 45 hours in a week, gross earnings are: ($665/$630).

IV. Case Analysis

Assume that G. Company decides to lease new equipment. The lease period is 4 years, and the economic life of the equipment is estimated to be 5 years. The present value of the lease payment is $190,000 which is equal to the fair market value of the equipment. There is no transfer of ownership during the lease term. Please make an entry to record the transaction.

Reading Material

Advantages of Bonds

Have you ever heard co-workers talking around the water cooler about a hot tip on a bond? Tracking bonds can be about as thrilling as watching a chess match, whereas watching stocks can have some investors as excited as NFL fans during the Superbowl. But don't let the hype (or lack thereof) mislead you. Both stocks and bonds have their pros and cons, and in this article we will explain the advantages of bonds and why you might want to include them in your portfolio.

A Safe Haven for Your Money

Those just entering the investment scene are usually able to grasp the concepts underlying stocks and bonds. Essentially, the difference can be summed up in one phrase: debt vs. equity. That is, bonds represent debts, and stocks represent equity ownership. This difference is the reason behind the first main advantage of bonds: investing in debts, in general, is safer than equity. The reason for this is the priority that debtholders have over shareholders. If a company goes bankrupt, debtholders are ahead of shareholders in the line to get paid. In a worst-case scenario such as bankruptcy, the creditors (debtholders) usually get at least some of their money back, while shareholders often lose their entire investment.

In terms of safety, bonds from the government (treasury bonds) are considered "risk-free". (There are no stocks that are considered as such.) If capital preservation, which is a fancy term for "never losing any money", is your goal above all else, then a bond from a stable government is your best investment. Naturally, although bonds are safer as a general rule, that doesn't mean they are all completely safe. There are very risky bonds referred to as "junk bonds".

Slow and Steady-Predictable Returns

If history is any indication, stocks will outperform bonds in the long run. However, bonds outperform stocks at certain times in the economic cycle. It's not unusual at all for stocks to lose 10% or more in a year, so when bonds comprise a portion of your portfolio, they can help smooth out the bumps when a recession comes around.

There are always conditions in which we need security and predictability. Retirees, for instance, often rely on the predictable income generated by bonds. If your portfolio consists solely of stocks, it would be quite disappointing to retire two years into a bear market! By owning bonds, retirees are able to predict with a greater degree of certainty how much income they'll have in their golden years. An investor who still has many years until retirement has plenty of time to make up for any losses from periods of decline in equities.

Better than the Bank

Sometimes bonds are just the only decent option. The interest rates on bonds are typically greater than the rates paid by banks on savings accounts. As a result, if you are saving and you don't need the money in the short term, bonds will give you the greatest return without bringing too much risk.

College savings are a good example of funds you want to invest to help increase your savings and protect them from risk at the same time. Simply putting money in the bank is a start, but it's not going to give you any return. With bonds, aspiring college students (or their parents) can predict their investment earnings and determine the amount they'll have to contribute to accumulate their tuition nest egg by the time college rolls around.

How Much Should You Put in Bonds?

There really is no easy answer to this question. Quite often you'll hear an old rule that says investors should formulate their allocation by subtracting their age from 100. The resulting figure indicates the percentage of a person's assets that should be invested in stocks, with the rest spread between bonds and cash. According to this rule, a 20-year-old people should have 80% in stocks and 20% in cash and bonds, while someone who is 65 should have 35% of assets in stocks and 65% in bonds and cash. That being said, rules of thumb are just that. Determining the asset allocation of your portfolio involves many factors including your investing timeline, risk tolerance, future goals, perception of the market, and income. Unfortunately, exploring the various factors affecting risk is beyond the scope of this article.

Conclusion

Hopefully, we've cleared up some misconceptions about bonds and demonstrated when they are appropriate. The bottom line is that bonds are a safe and conservative investment. They provide a predictable stream of income when stocks perform poorly, and they are great vehicles to save your money when you don't want to put them at risk.

Notes

portfolio	*n.* 投资搭配，有价证券组合，产品组合，（部长或大臣的）职务，作品集
treasury bonds	国库债券
junk bonds	*n.* 垃圾债券，风险债券
bear market	空头市场，熊市
nest egg	为养老、应变等备用的储蓄，养老金，储备金
risk tolerance	*n.* 风险承受力

Discussion questions:

(1) According to the above article, what do stocks and bonds represent respectively?

(2) Why is investing in debt safer than investing in equity? What kind of priority do debt holders have over shareholders?

(3) In the long run, will stocks outperform bonds?

(4) Why is investing in bonds better than the bank?

(5) Assume that you are a 21-year-old college graduate, and you now have $15,000 for portfolio selection, how would you determine the asset allocation of your portfolio according to the old rule discussed in this article?

Unit 6

Owners' Equity

The only thing that gives me pleasure is to see my dividend coming in.

———*John D. Rockefeller*

Study Objectives

After studying this unit, you should be able to:

- Identify a corporation and its major characteristics.
- Make clear the differences between paid-in capital and retained earnings.
- Differentiate between common stock and preferred stock.
- Explain capital stock and dividends.

Feature Story

There is a company which was formed in 1903. In the early years the company had issued shares to the public in order to finance the company's quick growth. In 1916 the company decided to retain funds to support its expansion, rather than pay funds out to stockholders in the form of dividend. This made the shareholders claimed, but the company's reaction was firm and direct: if the shareholders couldn't think the same way, they would be got rid of. In 1919 the initiator of the company purchased 100% of the outstanding shares of the company for purpose of removing all the outside "interference". It was over 35 years before shares were again issued to the public.

Years later, the top management of the company decided to centralize decision making—to have more key decisions made by top management, rather than by division managers.

This company is Ford Motor Company. Today there are billions shares of publicly traded stock outstanding.

International Background Information

Equity refers to residual interest in the assets of an entity that remains after deducting its liabilities. In a business enterprise, the equity is the ownership interest. It is usually divided into three parts:

◇ Capital stock—the par or stated value of the shares issued. 　　　股本
◇ Additional paid-in capital—the excess of amounts paid in over the par or stated value. 　　　股本溢价，我国计入资本公积账户
◇ Retained earnings—the corporation's undistributed earnings. 　　　留存收益

The major disclosure requirements for capital stock are the authorized, issued, and outstanding par value amounts. The additional paid-in capital is usually presented in one amount, although subtotals are informative if the sources of additional capital are varied and material. The retained earnings section may be divided between the unappropriated (the amount that is usually available for dividend distribution) and restricted (e. g., by bond indentures or other loan agreements) amounts. In addition, any capital stock reacquired is shown as a reduction of stockholders' equity.　　　票面价值，面值

Notes

Equity refers to residual interest in the assets of an entity that remains after deducting its liabilities.
所有者权益是指企业资产扣除负债后，由所有者享有的剩余权益。

6.1　Capital Stock

Corporation

In a general sense, a corporation is a separate and distinct entity given many of the same legal rights as an natural person. This means that a corporation can open a bank account, own property and do business, all under its own name. Corporations must have at least one owner, but there is no upper limit.

The owners of a corporation are called shareholders or stock-

holders. The ownership interests of the shareholders are divided into units called stock, shares, or shares of stock. The primary advantage of a corporation is that its owners are not personally liable for the debts and liabilities of the corporation. For example, if a corporation gets sued and is forced into bankruptcy, the owners will not be required to pay the debts with their own money. If the assets of the corporation are not enough to cover the debts, the creditors cannot claim repayment from the stockholders, directors, or officers of the corporation.

A corporation is managed by a board of directors, which is responsible for making important business decisions and for controlling the general affairs of the corporation. Like representatives in Congress, directors are elected by the stockholders of the corporation. Officers, who run the daily works of the corporation, are appointed by the board of directors.

Whether a person can become the shareholder is decided by whether he buys the shares, and not by the personal relationship between he and other shareholders. Therefore, a corporation can swiftly, extensively and largely collect fund. Although capital in an unlimited company or in a limited liability company is demarcated as shares, these companies don't issue stocks, and shares can't be transferred freely. All the stocks issued and circulated on stock markets are issued by corporations.

Stock is also named capital stock. The amount of money and property contributed by stockholders is used as the financial foundation for a corporation. Share is the element which constitutes stock, and also the calculating unit of stock. In another word, the amount of money and property of a corporation, stock, is comprised of shares, and it is equal to the total sum of all shares.[1]

Capital stock includes common stock and preferred stock.

International Insight

In the United States, stockholders are treated equally as far as access to financial information. That is not always the case in other countries. For example, in Mexico, foreign investors as well as minority investors often have difficulty obtaining financial data. These restrictions are rooted in the habits of companies that for many years have been tightly controlled by a few stockholders and managers.

Common Stock

Common stock represents ownership in a corporation. A single share of stock is a piece of ownership of the corporation. If a corporation issues 10 shares of stock, each share represents 10 percent of its ownership. If the corporation issues 100 shares, each share represents 1 percent of the ownership. This share entitles the owner to a vote in corporate decisions as well as a piece of the profits of the company.² Of course, most companies issue millions of shares of stock, so each share represents only a tiny piece of the company. These shares are also able to be transferred, Which is what you are doing every time you place a trade.

Common stock dividends may be paid in cash, stock or property. The most common payment method is a cash dividend. The board of directors determines whether or not to pay dividends to common shareholders. Increases or reductions most frequently depend on how well the company is performing. In a weak economy, the company may even suspend dividends until its balance sheet improves.

Should the corporation issuing the stock go bankrupt and have to sell its assets, common stockholders will receive the assets, but only after all other creditors, bondholders and preferred stockholders receive them first.³

Rights of Common Stockholders:
• Vote in the election of board of directors at annual meeting.
• Share the corporate earnings through receipt of dividends.
• Keep same percentage ownership when new shares of stock are issued.
• Share in assets upon liquidation, in proportion to their holdings.

Preferred Stock

Preferred stock also represents ownership in a corporation. Preferred stock gives its owners certain preferences superior to those of common stock. The following rights are those most often associated with preferred stock issues.

- Preference as to dividends.
- Preference as to assets at liquidation.
- Convertible into common stock.

To obtain the above rights, preferred shareholders cannot vote or share other specified rights.

A preference as to dividends is not assurance that dividends will be paid. It is merely assurance that the stated dividend rate or amount applicable to the preferred stock must be paid before any dividends can be paid on the common stock.

Preferred stock may have either a par value or no-par value.

票面价值

Par value stock is capital stock that has been assigned a value per share in the corporate charter. The par value may be any amount selected by the corporation. Generally, par value is a very small amount that bears no relationship to its market price. For example, a company has a par value of $1.25, while its recent market price may have risen to $80 per share.

The dividend payments of preferred stock are a fixed percentage of the par. For example, if the par value of a stock share was $100 with a 6 percent annual dividend rate, the annual dividend would be $6 on that share. In recent years, some companies have also begun issued preferred shares with variable rates tied to interest rates.

Notes

1. In another word, the amount of money and property of a corporation, stock, is comprised of shares, and is equal to the total sum of all shares.

   这句的意思是：换句话说，股份公司的资金和财产总额，即股本，是由股份构成的，且等于全部股份金额的总和。

2. This share entitles the owner to a vote in corporate decisions as well as a piece of the profits of the

company.

as well as = in addition (to) 除……之外,也,同。翻译句子时,先翻译 as well as 后面的部分。

这句的意思是:这种股票使所有者除有权获得公司的一份利润外,还有权对公司的决策进行表决。

3. Should the corporation issuing the stock go bankrupt and have to sell its assets, common stockholders will receive the assets, but only after all other creditors, bondholders and preferred stockholders receive them first.

前半句是混合型虚拟语气的句式,使用了倒装结构,省略 if。正常的语序是:If the corporation issuing the stock should go bankrupt and have to sell its assets, 分词短语 issuing the stock 做定语,后置修饰 corporation。该句的意思是:

如果发行股票的公司破产且不得不卖掉它的资产,那么只有在其他所有的债权人、债券持有者和优先股的股东获得清算资产后,才轮到普通股的股东。

6.2　Retained Earnings

When a company **generates** a profit, the management has two choices: they can either pay it out to shareholders as a cash dividend, or **retain** the **earnings** and reinvest them in the business.

vt. 产生

vt. 留存/*n.* 收益

Typically, a portion of the profit is distributed to shareholders in the form of dividend. What gets left over is called retained earnings or retained capital.

When the executives decide that earnings should be retained, they have to account for them on the balance sheet under shareholder equity. This allows investors to see how much money has been put into the business over the years. If a company is **plowing all of its earnings back** into itself and doesn't enjoy significant growth, you can be sure that the stockholders would probably be better served if the board of directors declared a dividend.

以收益作为资本投资

Ultimately, the goal for any successful management is to create $1 in market value for every $1 of retained earnings.

When **sizing up** a company's fundamentals, investors need to look at how much capital is kept from shareholders. Making profits for shareholders ought to be the main objective for a **listed company** and, as such, investors tend to pay most attention to reported

判断,估量

上市公司

profits. Profits are important for sure, but what the company does with that money is equally important. Investors should look closely at how a company puts retained capital to use and generates a return on it.

International Insight

In Switzerland, companies are allowed to create income reserves. That is, they reduce income in the years with good profits by allocating it to reserves on the balance sheet. In less profitable years, they are able to reallocate from the reserves to improve income. This "smoothes" income across years.

Assignment

Ⅰ. Select the best answer for each of the following questions or uncompleted sentences.

(1) The fixed number is paid by equity investors, and they are the proprietors of the entity. The fixed number is _____. The profit generated by entity's management earned is _____.

 A. paid-in capital   B. retained earnings
 C. dividend   D. cash

(2) "Earnings" is another name for Net Profits. If earnings haven't been distributed as dividends, it should have been retained in the company. The name of this portion of number listed in the balance sheet is _____.

 A. paid-in capital   B. retained earnings
 C. dividend   D. cash

(3) The price of a company stock is the price people are willing to purchase. This is the market value. It _____ on the balance sheet.

 A. appears   B. doesn't appear
 C. doesn't change   D. maybe appear

(4) Stock splitting and stock dividends have the same effect. The "cash" will be _____. The "nondistributed earnings" will be _____. The market price of each share will be _____.

 A. increased   B. decreased
 C. unchanged   D. none of above

(5) Preferred stock may not have priority over common stock except in _____.

 A. voting   B. conversion

C. dividends   D. liquidate assets
(6) The owners of a limited company are called _____.
    A. shareholders   B. debenture holders
    C. directors   D. creditors

Ⅱ. Mark the correct items by "√" and the wrong items by "×".

(1) Shareholders' equity of a corporation is made up of paid-in capital and retained earnings. (   )
(2) The common stockholders can not vote in the election of board of directors at annual meeting. (   )
(3) Preferred stock pays a fixed dividend that is specified. (   )
(4) Retained earnings account is decreased by cash dividends, not by stock dividends. (   )
(5) A share dividend will increase a stockholder's equity in the corporation. (   )

Ⅲ. Study the brief cases and fill in the blanks.

(1) The account of retained earnings _____ with the increasing of the net income per period. Therefore, at the early time of some period, the retained earnings is ￥100,000, the dividends distributed in this period is ￥20,000, net income is ￥30,000, then retained earnings at the end of this period should be ￥_____.

(2) If ABC Company declared to issue dividend per share at ￥0.5, and the company has outstanding stock of 1,000,000, then the dividend should be ￥_____. The accounting entry which would have some influence caused by the recording of this distribution should be:

Dr. _____ _____
Cr. _____ _____

　　If ABC Company owned shares of 100,000 in its earlier stage, the market price was ￥200 per share. After the management of the business issued a 20% stock dividend, the amount of outstanding stock will be _____ [increased/decreased/unchanged]. Cash will be _____ [increased/decreased/unchanged]. The market price per share will be _____ [increased/decreased/unchanged].

(3) If ABC Company earns 25 cents a share in 2008 and ￥1.35 a share in 2018, then per-share earnings rose by ￥1.10. From 2008 to 2018, the company earned a total of ￥7.50 per share. Of the ￥7.50, ABC Company paid out ￥2 in dividends, and therefore had a retained earnings of ￥5.50 a share. Since the company's earnings per share in 2018 is ￥1.35, we know the ￥5.50 in retained earnings produced ￥1.10 in additional income in 2018. ABC Company's management earned a return of _____ in 2018 on the ￥5.50 a share in retained earnings.

Ⅳ. Case Analysis

Refer to the Feature Story of this unit, and consult more information about the history of Ford

Motor Company (www. Ford. Com), then discuss the following questions.

(1) Why did initiator Henry Ford choose to form a corporation rather than a sole proprietorship?

(2) Why did Ford Motor Company repurchase all of its shares?

(3) What are the advantages and disadvantages of organizing a corporation which are illustrated by Ford?

Reading Material

Risks in Investment

Low-Risk Investments

Classic low-risk investments are government stocks and bank deposits. The institutions aren't likely to go out of existence. And the investments are "capital guaranteed", meaning your balance can never drop below the amount you put in.

But even these classic low-risk investments carry the risk. When bank interest rates rise, you will be stuck with your money tied up at the lower interest rates at which you first invested. And not every fixed-interest investment is with a stable organization. Some providers may offer capital "guaranteed" products, but in fact no third party is guaranteeing the continuing financial power of the provider. That is to say, although there is a guarantee offered, there is no real guarantee. So investors must check that the guarantee and the person or institution offering it are both well-being. Any guarantee is only as good as those offering it.

High-Risk Investment

The classic high-risk investment is in shares of a small company which is newly listed on the stock exchange. Such a small company may easily go bankrupt, but the share price may soar.

On average, high-risk investors make more than low-risk ones. The stock market would reward them for taking a risk during a period, and sometimes making them lose totally. Even during the 1980s, the decade of the stock market crash, the whole earnings of shares outperformed lower-risk fixed interest and property investments.

From above, we learn the first basic rule relating to risk: "High risk equals high return". If you want to maximize your savings, take some risk with at least some of your money.

Keep in mind, while, the second rule relating to risk: diversify, or "Don't put all your eggs in one basket". This, to some extent, can prevent you from being hurt too badly if one company falls down. Research shows that you won't be rewarded with high returns for the all-egg-in-one-basket type of risk. In short, you're unwise not to spread your money around, as all the big financial institutions do. This means dividing your money among different types of investments—some in shares, some in property, some in bonds, etc. You can also invest in different groups and even different countries.

Notes

soar　　　　v. 暴涨（指股票）

diversify　　v. 多元化

Exercises:

Decide whether the statements are True（T）or False（F）according to the passage.

（1）Classic low-risk investments include government stocks, bank savings and buying shares issued by big companies. （　　）

（2）If providers are reliable, the guarantee they offered is surely reliable. （　　）

（3）The classic high-risk investment is in shares of a small listed company. （　　）

（4）Stock market is always rewarding those who would make a high-risk investment. （　　）

（5）If you really want to have more money, you should have some high-risk investments. （　　）

Unit 7 Revenues, Expenses and Profits

Study Objectives

After studying this unit, you should be able to:
- Understand the accounting revenues.
- Identify different types of revenues.
- Understand the accounting expenses and costs.
- Identify different types of expenses.
- Understand the accounting profits.
- Know how to calculate the accounting profits for the accounting period.

Feature Story

There is a couple who are both accountants. One day, the wife bought some cosmetics with the husband's salary and kept them in her records as: Non-operating revenue—cosmetics offered by husband. But her husband classified them in his account book as: repair expense—wife's cosmetic.

What are revenues? What are expenses?

In this unit, we'll introduce the connection among revenues, expenses and profits, and study how to calculate the profits of a company.

International Background Information

Definitions

◇ Revenues—inflows or other enhancements of assets of an entity or settlements of its liabilities during a period from delivering or producing goods, rendering services, or other activities that constitute the entity's ongoing major or central operations.[1]

◇ Expenses—outflows or other using-up of assets or incurrences of liabilities during a period from delivering or producing goods, rendering services, or other activities that constitute the entity's ongoing major or central operations.[2]

◇ Gains—increases in equity (net assets) from peripheral or incidental transactions of an entity except those that result from revenues or investments by owners.[3]

◇ Losses—decreases in equity (net assets) from peripheral or incidental transactions of an entity except those that result from expenses or distributions to owners.[4]

Revenues take many forms, such as sales, fees, interest, dividends and rents.[5] Expenses also take many forms, such as cost of goods sold, depreciation, interest, rent, salaries and wages, and taxes.[6] Gains and losses also are of many types, resulting from the sale of investments, sale of plant assets, settlement of liabilities, write-offs of assets due to obsolescence or casualty, and theft.

settlement of liabilities 清偿债务
obsolescence or casualty 废旧过时或事故
theft n. 偷盗

Notes

1. Revenues—inflows or other enhancements of assets of an entity or settlements of its liabilities during a period from delivering or producing goods, rendering services, or other activities that constitute the entity's ongoing major or central operations.
   收入是指在一定期间内,企业通过提供或生产商品、提供服务或其他日常主要经营活动而导致的资产的流入或其他形式的增加,或债务的偿还。

2. Expenses—outflows or other using-up of assets or incurrences of liabilities during a period from delivering or producing goods, rendering services, or other activities that constitute the entity's ongoing major or central operations.
   费用是指在一定期间内,企业通过提供或生产商品、提供服务或其他日常主要经营活动而导致的资产的流出或耗用,或者是债务的产生。

3. Gains—increases in equity (net assets) from peripheral or incidental transactions of an entity except those that result from revenues or investments by owners.
   利得是指通过非主要的或非经常性的交易而导致的,与收入和所有者投资无关的,所有者权益(净资产)的增加。

4. Losses—decreases in equity (net assets) from peripheral or incidental transactions of an entity except those that result from expenses or distributions to owners.

损失是指通过非主要的或非经常性的交易而导致的，与费用和所有者分配无关的，所有者权益（净资产）的减少。

5. Revenues take many forms, such as sales, fees, interest, dividends and rents.

   收入有很多种方式，例如销售、费用、利息、股利和租金。

6. Expenses also take many forms, such as cost of goods sold, depreciation, interest, rent, salaries and wages, and taxes.

   费用也有很多种方式，例如销售费用、折旧、利息、租金、薪酬与工资，以及税费。

7.1 Revenues

In business, revenues are the gross inflows of economic benefits arising in the course of the ordinary activities of an enterprise from such events as the sale of goods, the rendering of services and the use of enterprise assets by others. Revenue does not include amounts collected on behalf of third parties or clients.[1] Revenue growth is an important indicator of the market reception of a company's products and services. Enterprises shall rationally recognize revenue and account for the revenue on time. There are rules specifying when revenue should be recognized and counted in different situations as follows.

提供劳务

n. 指示器

adv. 理性地
vt. 详细说明

Prime Operating Revenues

主营业务收入

1. Sales Revenue

While an accountant confirms revenue, there are several conditions that must be noticed. Firstly, the enterprise must have transferred the significant risks and rewards to the buyer when he owns the goods. Secondly, the enterprise retains neither continuing managerial involvement to the degree usually associated with ownership nor effective control over the goods sold.[2] Thirdly, the economic benefits associated with the transaction will flow to the enterprise and the relevant amount of revenue and costs can be measured reliably.

adj. 相关的
adv. 可靠地

Revenue arising from the sale of goods should be determined in accordance with the amount stipulated in the contract or agreement signed by the enterprise and the buyer, or with an amount agreed between them.[3] The cash discounts ought to be recognized

vt. 规定

as an expense in the period in which they are actually incurred. Otherwise, sales allowances should be recorded as a reduction of revenue in the period when the allowances are actually made.

2. Service Revenue

When services provided start and complete within the same accounting year, revenue should be recognized at the time of completion of the services. To calculate the revenue, the conditions of transactions and computing methods are very important. The accountant needs to make sure that the total amount of revenue and costs of completion of the services provided can be measured reliably, and the economic benefits associated with the transaction will flow to the enterprise. Appropriate methods to determine the stage of completion of the services are as follows:

- To survey work performed.
- To check the proportion of services performed to the total services to be performed, or the proportion of costs incurred to the estimated total costs.
- To determine total revenue arising from the rendering of services in accordance with the amount stipulated in the contract or agreement.

Other Operating Revenues

Revenues arising from the use of enterprise assets by others include revenues resulted from wrappage lease and remised right of assets. These revenues should be measured according to the period and charging method as stipulated in the relevant contract or agreement by the following conditions: the economic benefits associated with the transaction will flow to the enterprise, and the amount of the revenue can be measured reliably.

Interest Revenue

Interest should be measured on the applicable interest rate and the length of time for which the enterprise's cash is used by others.

adj. 适当的

n. 比例

其他业务收入

n. 包装材料/*vt.* 让与

利息收入

adj. 适用的,适当的

Unit 7 Revenues, Expenses and Profits

Notes

1. Revenue does not include amounts collected on behalf of third parties or clients.

   on behalf of 指代表……，该句的意思是：

   收入不包括为第三方或客户代收的款项。

2. …the enterprise retains neither continuing managerial involvement to the degree usually associated with ownership nor effective control over the goods sold.

   neither…nor…是 retain（保留）的并列宾语，意思是"既没有保留……也没有保留……"

   to the degree…到某种程度，associated with ownership 是 involvement 的后置定语。该句的意思是：

   企业既不能保留通常在某种程度上与所有权相联系的继续管理权，也不能保留对已售出商品的有效控制权。

3. Revenue arising from the sale of goods should be determined in accordance with the amount stipulated in the contract or agreement signed by the enterprise and the buyer, or with an amount agreed between them.

   in accordance with 与……一致，依照；should be 应该，虚拟语气，当双方签订合同时，企业应该……。该句的意思是：

   销售商品的收入应按企业与买方签订的合同或协议的金额或者双方同意的金额来确定。

7.2 Expenses

Expense can be a general term for an outgoing payment made by a business or individual. In accounting, the term expense has two meanings:

- Period expenses.
- Capital expenditure or expenditure subject to depreciation.

In order to tell one from another clearly, we use two accounting technical terms—— "Expense" and "Costs". This unit discusses period expenses only.

Expense is the outflow of economic benefits from the enterprise arising from ordinary activities such as sales of goods and rendering of services. General and administrative expenses incurred by enterprise's organizing production and operation, financial expenses, purchase expenses and sales expenses for selling

期间费用

products and providing services, shall be directly accounted for as period expenses in the current profit and loss. Period expenses should be directly charged to the income statement for the current period. Expenses are the opposite of revenues.

Period expenses should be separately presented in the income statement.

(1) **Selling Expenses** are expenses incurred during the sales process, including freight charges, handling fees, packaging, insurance, exhibition and advertising expenses, as well as operating expenses of sales structures (sales network, after-sales services network, etc.) including payroll and benefits, other expenses in the nature of wages, and business expenses. For a commodity trading firm, selling expenses also include expenses arising from the process of purchasing merchandises.

(2) **Administrative Expenses** are expenses incurred in organizing and managing the operating activities of an enterprise. Administration expenses include expenses incurred by the board of directors administration department, head office expenses (including administration department's payroll, costs of repair and maintenance, materials consumed, amortization of consumables, office expenses and business traveling expenses, etc.), union dues, unemployment insurance, labor insurance, directors' fees, professional fees, consulting fees (including fees for advisors), litigation expenses, entertainment expenses, rates on property, transportation tax, land-use tax, stamp duties, technology transfer fees, expenses for use of mineral resources, amortization of intangible assets, training fees, research and development costs, sewage charges, inventories loss or excess during a stock-take (except losses on inventories that should be included as non-operating expenses), provision for bad debts and provision for decline in value of inventories as well.

(3) **Financial** Expenses are expenses incurred by an enterprise in raising funds required for operations. Financial expenses include interest expenses that should be included as period expenses (less interest income), exchange losses (less exchange

gains), and other relevant handling charges.

The expenses paid in current period but attributable to the current and future periods shall be distributed and accounted for in current and future periods. The expenses attributable to the current period but not yet paid in current period shall be recognized as accrued expenses of the current period.

7.3 Profits

Definition and Classification of Profits

Profit, generally defined, is the return received on a business undertaking after all operating expenses have been met. However, the exact method of calculation differs between accountants and economists. Economists usually define profit as revenue less the opportunity costs. In the sense of accounting, profit is the operating result of an enterprise in an accounting period, including operating profit, net investment profit and net non-operating income.

Operating profit equals to income from the principal business operations less related costs and business taxes, plus profit from other business operations, less selling expenses, administrative expenses and financial expenses.

Net investment profit means a net amount equal to gains from external investments less the investment losses incurred and any provision for impairment losses on investments.[1]

Net non-operating income is the balance of non-operating income after deducting non-operating expenses. Non-operating income and expenses have no direct relationship with the production operations of an enterprise. Non-operating income includes excess found in a fixed asset count, net profit on disposal of fixed assets, net profit on disposal of intangible assets, net income from penalties, etc. Non-operating expenses include loss found in a fixed asset count, net loss on disposal of fixed assets, net loss on disposal of intangible assets, loss on debt restructuring, provisions for impairment losses on intangible assets, fixed assets and construction in progress, penalty payments, donation payments, and abnormal losses, etc. Non-operating income and non-operating expenses should be accounted for separately and be presented in the income statement as separate items.²

When you look into the income statement, you will find another two important profits on the statement, gross profit and net profit. Gross profit is the residual after deduction of all money costs. It is the net profit before tax. Net profit after tax is the profit after the deduction of income tax. If the figure is a positive number, we can say the enterprise earns a profit, in the contract, it is in an undesirable situation.

Generally, an enterprise should calculate its profit on a monthly basis. If an enterprise has difficulties in preparing monthly profit calculations, it may calculate its profit on a quarterly or annual basis.³ If it has an earning in the current period, the next thing is to make an appropriation plan.

Profit Distribution

Profit available for appropriation comprises net profit realized in the current period, the balance of any inappropriate profit at the beginning of the year (or deducts the balance of any accumulated losses at the beginning of the year) and any other balances transferred into profit available for appropriation. They should be appropriated in the following order:

• The statutory surplus reserve.

• The discretionary surplus reserve as required.

• The amounts for other reserves in accordance with laws and regulations.

A profit appropriation plan proposed by the board of directors or a similar body should first be reflected in the profit appropriation statement for the year reported upon, and then put forward for approval by the shareholders' meeting or a meeting of a similar body.

After all these sequences, profit available for distribution to the investors should be appropriated. First, pay the cash dividend to the shareholders of preferred stock. Next is (cash) dividend

---

n. 捐赠品，捐款，贡献

利润总额，毛利润

adj. 不受欢迎的

净利润
未分配利润

法定盈余公积
任意盈余公积

n. 次序，顺序，序列

on common stock. The last is (stock) dividend paid to common shareholders which is an increase of share capital issued as bonus shares.

After making the above distributions, the balance of the profit is inappropriate profit, which may be appropriated in subsequent periods.

Notes

1. Net investment profit means a net amount equal to gains from external investments less the investment losses incurred and any provision for impairment losses on investments.
   该句的意思是：投资净利润是指企业对外投资所取得的收益减去发生的投资损失和计提的投资减值准备后的净额。

2. Non-operating income and non-operating expenses should be accounted for separately and be presented in the income statement as separate items.
   account for 说明，占，解决，得分。
   be presented 与 be accounted 并列，承接前面的 should。该句的意思是：
   营业外收入和营业外支出应当分别核算，并在利润表中分列项目反映。

3. If an enterprise has difficulties in preparing monthly profit calculations, it may calculate its profit on a quarterly or annual basis.
   该句的意思是：
   如果企业按月计算利润有困难，可以按季或者按年计算利润。

Assignment

Ⅰ. Select the best answer for each of the following questions or uncompleted sentences.

(1) If a company earned the revenues of $800,000 and incurred the expenses of $750,000, then its net earnings are _____.
   A. $1,550,000   B. $50,000
   C. $800,000   D. $750,000

(2) Which of the following can be recognized as revenues? _____.
   A. Amortization of intangible assets
   B. Freight charges   C. Sales returns
   D. Cash discount   E. Interest income

(3) Which of the following is not true? _____.
   A. Interest revenue should be measured based on the length of time
   B. Sales allowances should be recorded as a reduction of revenues

C. Sales returns should be recorded as a reduction of revenues

D. An appropriate method needn't to determine the stage of completion of the services

E. None of the above

(4) Which of the following is not true according to the formula?_____.

$$Profits = TR - TC = (AR \times Q) - (AC \times Q) = Q \times (AR - AC)$$

A. TR ＝ Total Revenues
B. Q ＝ Quantity sold
C. AC ＝ Alternating Current
D. AR ＝ Average Revenues

(5) Which of the following shows the details of the company's activities involving cash during a period of time?_____.

A. Income statement
B. Statement of financial position
C. Balance sheet
D. Revenues – Costs ＝ Profits
E. None of the above

(6) A certain transaction affecting only two accounts causes a liability to decrease by a certain amount. Which one of the following could not be another effect of the same transaction? _____.

A. A paid-in capital account is increased by the same amount

B. An expense account is increased by the same amount

C. An asset account is decreased by the same amount

D. A revenue account is increased by the same amount

Ⅱ. Mark the correct items by "√" and the wrong items by "×".

(1) Costs, prices, sales volume, profits, and return on investment are all accounting measurements. ( )

(2) A present reduction in cash required to generate revenues is called an expense. ( )

(3) Accrual accounting is done by recognizing revenues when earned and expenses incurred. ( )

(4) Revenues increase owner's equity. ( )

(5) If revenues exceed expenses for the same accounting period, the entity is deemed to suffer a loss. ( )

(6) Cash flows from financing activities are the cash effects of revenue and expense transactions that are included in the income statement. ( )

Ⅲ. Case Analysis

Let's analyze the Sikly Company's following expenditures in May 2018:

(1) Paid relevant handling charges 3,000 dollars for purchasing the long-term bond.

(2) When sold goods, Sikly Company had given the customer 200 dollars sales allowance, and 300 dollars cash discount.

(3) Paid the business entertainment expenses 5,000 dollars, among them 4,000 dollars belonging to

the sale department, the rest belonging to the management section.

(4) Paid 22,000 dollars auditing fee.

(5) Paid 80,000 dollars advertising expense, 2,400 dollars business traveling expenses for sale department, and 1,200 dollars for office expenses.

(6) The loss of fixed assets found in a fixed asset count was 6,200 dollars.

(7) Expended 4,500 dollars to pay for the short-term loan interest.

(8) Expended 2,500 dollars for short-term investments falling price reserves.

Analyze:

(1) Financial expenses include interest expenses and other relevant handling charges. Financial expenses increase 3,000 dollars.

(2) The accountant ought to recognize the cash discounts as an expense in the period in which they are actually incurred. Otherwise, sales allowances should be recorded as a reduction of revenue in the period in which the allowances are actually made. Financial expenses increase 300 dollars.

(3) Administrative expenses include entertainment expenses. Administrative expenses increase 5,000 dollars.

(4) Administrative expenses include professional fees. Administrative expenses increase 22,000 dollars.

(5) Selling expenses are expenses incurred during the sales process, including advertising expenses, and operating expenses of sales structures including payroll and benefits, other expenses in the nature of wages, and business expenses.

Selling expenses increase 83,600 dollars. (80,000 + 2,400 + 1,200 = 83,600)

(6) Non-operating expenses include loss of fixed assets found in a fixed asset count. Non-operating expenses increase 6,200 dollars.

(7) Financial expenses include interest expenses. Financial expenses increase 4,500 dollars.

(8) Net investment profit represents a net amount equal to gains from external investments less the investment losses incurred and any provision for impairment losses on investments. Net investment profit decreases 2,500 dollars.

Please analyze the change in amounts of the expenses and the net investment profit in May 2018.

Reading Material

What Is Business Income Tax?

Just as the IRS (Internal Revenue Service) taxes individuals' earnings from their jobs, it also taxes the income of a business. If the income has anything to do with your business, whether or not that business is full time, part time, or occasional, that income is business income. The IRS says:

If there is a connection between any income you receive from your business, the income is business income. A connection exists if it is clear that the payment of income would not have been made if you did not have the business.

You can have business income even if you are not involved in the activity on a regular full-time basis. Income from work you do on the side in addition to your regular job can be business income. (IRS Publication 334: Tax Guide for Small Business for Individuals Who Use Schedule C or C-EZ).

Business income is generally subject to federal, state, and local income taxes. If you are running a business, you will need to fill out a tax return each year and send it to them by the due date. You need to account for income tax on your profits and the expenses you may deduct from your income. During the tax year you must generally pay interim tax, which is a periodical income tax for this tax year. For example, if your business got assistance this year, you must pay tax on this part this year. You have to pay income tax on your net profit for the year. To work out your net profit, you must deduct your business expenses from your income for the year.

In calculating income taxes payable to governmental units, businesses must complete the income tax returns including a statement showing the amount of net income subject to tax. In general, the form and content of the income tax return are similar to those of the accounting income statement.

Despite of that, there are still differences between the basic objectives of measuring taxable income and accounting income exists. Because the income tax is computed in accordance with prescribed tax regulations and rules, while accounting income in the income statement is measured up to the generally accepted accounting principles. Timing differences and permanent differences are the most importance types. When calculating income tax, you must keep track of them frequently. For example: The FASB concluded that inter-period tax allocation was required to account for the tax effects of transaction which involve timing differences, and was not appropriate for permanent differences.

At the end of it, you also need to learn about which income tax rate applies to your type of business, when income tax returns should be sent in and what income tax returns to use.

Exercises:

Decide whether the statements are True (T) or False (F) according to the passage.

(1) Business income tax is the tax on profits made by companies. (　　)

(2) During the tax year you must generally pay provisional tax, which is the tax paid by a company in advance of its main corporation tax payments. (　　)

(3) The income tax return is the same as the income statement. (　　)

(4) You can have business income even if you are not involved in the activity on a regular part-time basis. (　　)

(5) When calculating income tax, you must keep track of two types of differences. One is periodic differences, the other is permanent differences. (　　)

Unit 8　Balance Sheet

Study Objectives

After studying this unit, you should be able to:
- Explain what a Balance Sheet is.
- Understand the components of a balance sheet.
- Understand the basis of a balance sheet.
- Prepare a balance sheet.

Feature Story

The Bank of Paris, which is the first commercial bank in the world, was established in 1763 with its headquarters in London. In the end of 1995, this most famous old-line commercial bank went bankruptcy.

What made this old brand bank go to the dead end? There was a rather classic problem as well as the problem of the domination inside the bank—the chairman of the board of directors, Peter Barlin, didn't take the Balance Sheet seriously. He once said in a speech: It was really naive and ignorant if one thought he could enhance the understanding of a Group by revealing more data of a balance sheet. Satirically, the Bank of Paris bankrupted in less than a year after he delivered his "brilliant views", which was far beyond his expectation. The bank paid a distressing price due to his not attaching importance to the reading of balance sheet. As a matter of fact, the bank's being bankrupt could absolutely be avoided. Banks had to compile the balance sheets everyday. Had the superior administers pay close attention to the balance sheet, they would have known what had happened in the bank, and had they taken some remedial measures accordingly, the bank wouldn't have closed down.

Though Balance Sheet reflect the data which is at a specific moment in time, if we take it into account, know about it and make full use of it, it can do great contribution to our management.

International Background Information

Limitations of the Balance Sheet

The bankruptcy of the seventh largest U. S. company, Enron, highlights the fact that not all items of importance are reported in the balance sheet. In Enron's case, it had certain off-balance-sheet financing obligations which were not disclosed in the main financial statements.

资产负债表外/财务义务
vt. 披露
财务报表

Some of the major limitations of the balance sheet are:

◇ Most assets and liabilities are stated at historical cost. As a result, the information reported in the balance sheet has higher reliability but is subject to the criticism that a more relevant current fair value is not reported.

历史成本

公允价值

◇ Judgments and estimates are used in determining many of the items reported in the balance sheet.

◇ The balance sheet necessarily omits many items that are of financial value to the business but cannot be recorded objectively. For example, the knowledge and skill of Intel's employees in developing new computer chips are undoubtedly the company's most significant asset. However, because it is difficult to reliably measure the value of employees and other intangible assets (such as customer base, research superiority, and reputation), these items are not recognized in the balance sheet.

vt. 遗漏，省略
adv. 客观地

n. 商誉，信誉

Notes

The bankruptcy of the seventh largest U. S. company, Enron, highlights the fact that not all items of importance are reported in the balance sheet.

曾是美国七巨头之一的安然公司的破产事件揭露了这样一个事实：资产负债表并没有披露所有的重要事项。

安然（Enron）曾是美国最大的能源交易商，全球最大的能源巨头公司之一，在 2001 年《财富》世界 500 强排名第七位。然而，2001 年年底，安然公司正式宣布破产。从公开的资料看，安然在会计处理上存在以下重大错误：①未将巨额债务入账；②将未来期间不确定的收益计入本期收益，未充分披露其不确定性；③公司在合同上利用某种安排，在账上多记应收项目和股东权益 12 亿美元；④会计报表披露不便于投资者理解，不够充分，有故意误导之嫌。

8.1　Concept of the Balance Sheet

What Is a Balance Sheet?

A balance sheet is a snapshot of a business financial condition at a specific moment in time, usually at the close of an accounting period. The reason why it is referred to as a "snapshot" is that it gives you a fairly clear picture of the business at that moment, but does not in itself reveal how the business arrived there or where it's going next.[1] The balance sheet is not the whole story — you must also look at the information from each of the other financial statements to get the most benefit from the data. It together with the income statement, makes up the cornerstone of any company's financial statements.

Who Wants to See Your Balance Sheet?

Many people and organizations are interested in the financial situation of your company. Managers, creditors and investors all need to familiarize themselves with the assets, liabilities, and equity of a company. You, of course, want to know about the progress of your enterprise and what's happening to your livelihood. However, your creditors also want assurance that you will be able to pay them when they ask. Prospective investors are looking for a solid company to bet their money on, and they want financial information to help them make a sound decision. Your management group also requires detailed financial data, and the labor unions (if applicable) want to know whether your employees are getting a fair share of your business earnings. The balance sheet is the place to find all this handy information.

What Is the Balance Sheet Used for?

When someone, whether a creditor or investor, asks you how your company is doing, you'll want to have the answer ready and documented. The way to show off the success of your company is the balance sheet. The balance sheet is a documented report of your company's assets and obligations as well as the net equity at a given point in time.

It is a cumulative record that reflects the result of all recorded accounting transactions since your enterprise was formed. With a properly prepared balance sheet, you can know if your business has more or less value, if your debts are higher or lower, and if your working capital is higher or lower, at the end of each accounting period.[2]

By analyzing your balance sheet, investors, creditors and others can assess your solvency ability. The balance sheet also shows the composition of assets and liabilities, the relative proportions of debt and equity and the amount of earnings that you have had to retain. Collectively, this information will be used by external parties to help assess your company's financial status, which is required by both lending institutions and investors before they will allot any money toward your business.

adj. 累积的
会计事项

n. 偿付能力

Notes

1. The reason why it is referred to as a "snapshot" is that it gives you a fairly clear picture of the business at that moment, but does not in itself reveal how the business arrived there or where it's going next.

   前面的这个分句是含有 why 引导的定语从句的复合句。其主句的结构是 The reason…is that it gives you…at that moment。后面的分句中的 how 和 where 引导的句子是 reveal 的宾语从句。该句的意思是：

   资产负债表之所以被认为是一个"快照"，是因为它给了你一张企业在那个时刻相当清晰的画面，但它本身并没有揭示企业是怎样达到这个状况或者它下一步会怎么样。

2. With a properly prepared balance sheet, you can know if your business has more or less value, if your debts are higher or lower, and if your working capital is higher or lower, at the end of each accounting period.

   if your business has more or less value, if your debts are higher or lower, if your working capital is higher or lower 是谓语动词 know 的三个并列宾语从句。该句的意思是：

   如果有了正确编制的资产负债表，你就能知道在每一个会计期末你公司的价值是更多了还是更少了，你的债务是更高了还是更低了，你的实收资本是更高了还是更低了。

8.2 Contents and Formats of the Balance Sheet

A balance sheet comprises assets, liabilities, and owners' or stockholders' equity.

In general, the balance sheet is divided into two parts based on the following equation:

Assets = Liabilities + Owners' Equity

The table below can illustrate in detail the components of the balance sheet.

Left Hand Side	Right Hand Side
Assets	Liabilities & Owners' Equity
Current Assets—include cash, accounts receivable, and other assets that can be converted into cash relatively quickly	**Current Liabilities**—include a company's liabilities that will come due within the next 12 months
Property, Plant and Equipment (Fixed Assets)—long-term operating assets (less depreciation on these assets)	**Non-current Liabilities**—debts not maturing in the next 12 months. A good example is outstanding bonds that don't mature for several years
Intangible Assets—include the long-term assets that are not physical in nature	**Owners' Equity**—the economic benefit which the owners enjoy in the company's assets
Total Assets	Total Liabilities & Owners' Equity

Assets

Three types of assets are included in the balance sheet: current assets, property/plant/equipment, and intangible assets.

- **Current Assets** have a life span of one year or less, meaning they can easily be converted into cash. All current assets are short-term, highly liquid assets that can easily be converted into cash and used as currency.

• **Property, Plant and Equipment** (Fixed Assets), known as long-term assets, have a life span of over one year. They can refer to tangible assets such as machinery, computers, buildings and land. Depreciation is calculated and deducted from these types of assets.

• **Intangible Assets** also are long-term assets, such as goodwill, patent and copyright, while these assets are not physical in nature.

Liabilities

The liabilities are on the other side of the balance sheet. These are the financial obligations a company owes to outside clients. Like assets, they can be classified into current liabilities and non-current liabilities, namely long-term liabilities.

• **Current Liabilities** are typically paid within one year or less, and are therefore paid with current assets. Because current assets pay for current liabilities, the ratio between the two is important: a company should have enough of the former to cover the latter.

• **Non-Current Liabilities** are any debts or obligations owed by the business that are due more than one year out from the current date.

Owners' Equity

Owners' equity (Stockholders' equity) is the initial amount of money invested into a business. If a company decides to reinvest its net earnings (after taxes) into the company, at the end of the fiscal year, the retained earnings will be restated from the income statement onto the balance sheet here. The sum of the two figures represents a company's total net worth.

vt. 再投资于

Owners' equity is usually divided into three parts:

• Capital Stock—the par or stated value of the shares issued.

• Additional Paid-in Capital—the excess of amounts paid in over the par or stated value.

- Retained Earnings—the corporation's undistributed earnings.

International Insight

An example of the stockholders' equity section:

ABC Corporation
(in thousands)

Stockholders' Equity	
Preferred Stock, no par value, 1,000,000 shares authorized	
125,000 shares issued and outstanding	$31,250
Common Stock, $0.50 par value, 25,000,000 shares authorized	
10,125,006 shares issued and outstanding	$5,062
Additional Paid-in Capital	$12,360
Retained Earnings	$65,186
Total Stockholders' Equity	$113,858

In order to balance the balance sheet, total assets on one side have to equal total liabilities plus owners' equity on the other.

8.3 How to Prepare the Balance Sheet

Financial reports are the means to transmit useful information to users. The preparation of balance sheet is based on the data and information of the daily accounting operation and is a process of reaffirming them. A complete balance sheet should be composed of the followings.

- **Title**

In practice, the most widely used title is Balance Sheet, however Statement of Financial Position is also acceptable. When the presentation includes more than one time period, the title "Balance Sheets" should be used.

vt. 重申，再肯定

财务状况表

- **Heading**

In addition to the statement title, the heading of the balance sheet should include the legal name of the company and the date or dates the statement is presented. For example:

XYZ Corporation
Balance Sheet
December 31, 2018

- **Format**

There are two basic ways the balance sheet can be arranged. In Account Form, the assets are listed on the left-hand side, and the total figure equals the sum of liabilities and owners' equity on the right-hand side. Another format is Report Form, in which the assets are listed at the top of the page and followed by liabilities and owners' equity. By international convention, most businesses use the Balance Sheet in Account Form.

n. 格式

账户式

报告式

n. 惯例

The balance sheet is constructed in Report Form as follows.

Alpha Sales Company
Balance Sheet
December 31, 2018 (Simplified)

Assets	
Current Assets	$2,572
Property, Plant and Equipment (Fixed Assets)	$11,111
Other Assets	$1,210
Total Assets	**$14,893**
Liabilities and Owners' Equity	
Current Liabilities	$645
Long-term Liabilities	$4,000
Total Liabilities	**$4,645**
Owners' Equity	**$10,248**
Total Liabilities and Owners' Equity	**$14,893**

This is the example of balance sheet in Account Form.

Alpha Sales Company
Balance Sheet
December 31, 2018

Assets		Liabilities and Owners' Equity	
Current Assets		**Current Liabilities**	
Cash	$695	Accounts Payable	$520
Accounts Receivable	$1,237	Wages Payable	$125
Inventory	$580	**Total Current Liabilities**	**$645**
Prepaid Insurance	$60	**Non-Current Liabilities**	
Total Current Assets	**$2,572**	Bank Loan Payable	$4,000
Non-current Assets		**Total Non-Current Liability**	**$4,000**
Equipment	$19,823	**Total Liabilities**	**$4,645**
Less: Accumulation Depreciation	$8,712	**Owners' Equity**	
Net Value of Property, Plant and Equipment (Fixed Assets)	$11,111	Capital Stock	$7,208
		Retained Earnings	$3,040
Patents	$1,210	**Total Owners' Equity**	**$10,248**
Total Non-Current Assets	$12,321	**Total Liabilities & Owners' Equity**	**$14,893**
Total Assets	**$14,893**		

The formats of balance sheets can be different, but their preparing methods are the same as follows.

Beta Sales Company
Balance Sheet
December 31, 2018

Assets		
Current Assets		
Cash	$×× ×	Compute and fill in the sheet according to the balance of several general ledgers, including cash on hand, cash in banks, and cash equivalents
Notes Receivable (N/R)	$×× ×	Fill in the sheet directly according to the balance of general ledger
Accounts Receivable (A/R)	$×× ×	Compute and fill according to the balance of subsidiary ledger
Less: Reserve for Bad Debts	$×× ×	Fill in the sheet directly according to the balance of general ledger

（续）

Inventory（Inv.）	$×× ×	Compute and fill in the sheet according to the balance of several general ledgers, composed of merchandise inventory, unfinished products, raw materials, supplies and so on
Prepaid Expenses	$×× ×	Fill in the sheet directly according to the balance of general ledger
Long-Term Investments in Bonds (to be matured within a year)	$×× ×	Compute and fill in the sheet upon the analysis of the balance between subsidiary ledger and general ledger
Total Current Assets	$×× ×	
Non-Current Assets		
Long-Term Investments	$×× ×	Calculated and filled by the balance of general ledger and subsidiary ledger. Here the portion that will be matured within a year reflected in the relevant subsidiary ledger should be subtracted from the balance of long-term investments in general ledger
Vehicles	$×× ×	
Furniture and Fixtures	$×× ×	
Equipment	$×× ×	Fill in the sheet directly according to the balance of general ledger
Buildings	$×× ×	
Less: Accumulated Depreciation	$×× ×	
Land	$×× ×	
Total Property, Plant and Equment (Fixed Assets)	$×× ×	
Research and Development	$×× ×	
Patents	$×× ×	Fill in the sheet directly according to the balance of general ledger
Copyrights	$×× ×	
Total Non-Current Assets	$×× ×	
Total Assets	$×× ×	
Liabilities and Owners' Equity		
Current Liabilities		
Accounts Payable	$×× ×	Compute and fill according to the balance of subsidiary ledger
Sales Taxes Payable	$×× ×	
Accrued Wages Payable	$×× ×	Fill in the sheet directly according to the balance of general ledger
Short-Term Notes Payable	$×× ×	
Short-Term Bank Loan Payable	$×× ×	

（续）

Total Current Liabilities	$×× ×	
Non-Current Liabilities		
Long-Term Notes Payable	$×× ×	Compute and fill in the sheet upon the analysis of the balance between subsidiary ledger and general ledger. Here the reflected portion that will be matured within a year in the relevant subsidiary ledger should be subtracted from the balance of long-term loan in general ledger
Mortgage Payable	$×× ×	
Total Non-Current Liabilities	$×× ×	
Total Liabilities	$×× ×	
Owners' Equity		
Capital Stock	$×× ×	Fill in the sheet directly according to the balance of general ledger
Retained Earnings	$×× ×	Compute and fill according to the balance of subsidiary ledger
Total Owners' Equity	$×× ×	
Total Liabilities and Owners' Equity	$×× ×	

Assignment

I. Select the best answer for each of the following questions or uncompleted sentences.

(1) **Please select the items which do not belong to the balance sheet.** _____.

    A. Long-term investments   B. Accounts receivable

    C. Income tax expense   D. Retained earnings

(2) **Please select the component which should be deducted from the value of property, plant and equipment.** _____.

    A. Merchandise inventory   B. Income tax payable

    C. Accumulated depreciation   D. Retained earnings

(3) **Who dose not want to see your balance sheet?** _____.

    A. Creditor   B. Investor

    C. Manager   D. Customer

(4) **In general, which is the basis of preparing a balance sheet?** _____.

    A. Assets = Liabilities + Owners' Equity

    B. Assets − Liabilities = Owners' Equity

    C. Profits = Revenues − Expenses

D. Revenues = Profits + Expenses

(5) **The format of a balance sheet is not comprised as _____ .**

A. assets are listed on the left-hand side and totalled to equal the sum of liabilities and stockholders' equity on the right-hand side

B. assets are listed on the left-hand side and deducted total liabilities to equal stockholders' equity on the right-hand side

C. assets are listed at the top of the page and totalled to equal the sum of following liabilities and stockholders' equity

D. assets are listed at the top of the page and deducted total liabilities to equal stockholders' equity

Ⅱ. Case Analysis

During the year 2018, in ABC Company the following items took place:

(1) Issued 300,000 shares of $1 par value common stock.

(2) Purchased equipment for $50,000.

(3) Sold equipment costing $40,000 with a book value of $13,000 for $14,000.

(4) Paid $18,000 on accounts payable.

(5) Sold goods for $500,000 on account with a cost of $400,000.

(6) Purchased raw material for $100,000 but unclaimed deposit.

(7) Collected $16,000 of accounts receivable.

(8) Purchased a $15,000 machine, with paying $2,000 in cash, and issued a note payable for the remaining $13,000.

(9) Paid interest for $5,000.

(10) All depreciation expense, $11,000, is in the selling expense category.

(11) Paid salaries and wages for $50,000.

There is the company's balance sheet ended in December 31, 2017 for comparison. Please help ABC Company preparing a balance sheet for the year 2018.

ABC Company
Comparative Balance Sheet
December 31, 2017

Assets	
Cash	$42,485
Accounts Receivable	$165,024
Merchandise Inventory	$489,713
Property, Plant and Equipment	$1,100,800

(续)

Less: Accumulated Depreciation	$341,200
Total Assets	**$1,456,822**
Liabilities and Owners' Equity	
Accounts Payable	$147,530
Notes Payable	
Wages Payable	$50,000
Income Taxes Payable	$500
Bonds Payable	$500,000
Total Liabilities	**$698,030**
Owners' Equity	
Common Stock	$300,000
Retained Earnings	$458,792
Total Owners' Equity	**$758,792**
Total Liabilities and Owners' Equity	**$1,456,822**

Reading Material

Balance Sheet Analysis

A thorough analysis of a company's balance sheet is extremely important for both stock and bond investors.

The analysis of a balance sheet can identify potential liquidity problems. These may signify the company's inability to meet financial obligations. An investor could also spot the degree to which a company is leveraged, or indebted. An overly leveraged company may have difficulties raising future capital. Even more severe, they may be headed towards bankruptcy. These are just a few of the danger signs that can be detected with careful analysis of a balance sheet. All ratios are derived from balance sheet data.

1. **Quick Ratio**

  = (Cash + Accounts Receivable)/Current Liabilities

The Quick Ratio indicates liquid assets available to cover current debts. It is also known as the Acid Ratio. This is a "harsher" version of the Current Ratio, which balances short-term liabilities against cash and liquid instruments. Generally, any value of less than 1 to 1 suggests an over-reliance on inventory or other current assets to pay off short-term debt.

2. **Current Ratio**

  = Current Assets/Current Liabilities

The Current Ratio measures current assets available to cover current liabilities, a test of near-term solvency. The ratio indicates to what extent cash on hand and disposable assets are enough to pay off near term liabilities. Higher ratios indicate a better buffer between current obligations and a firm's ability to pay them. The quality of current assets is a critical factor in interpreting this analysis.

3. Current Assets to Cash

= Current Assets/Cash

This ratio reflects the number of times that current assets turn over in a year. As a comparison to sales, it is a less stringent measure of liquidity than the current asset turnover.

4. Inventory Turnover

= Cost of Sales/Average Inventory

Related financial Ratio: Days in Inventory = 365/(Cost of Sales/Average Inventory)

Average Inventory = (Beginning Inventory + Ending Inventory)/2

This financial ratio measures the number of times inventory is turned over during the year. High inventory turnover suggests good level of liquidity. Conversely it can indicate a shortage of needed inventory for sales. Low inventory turnover can indicate poor liquidity, overstocking, or more optimistically, a planned inventory buildup.

Days in Inventory measures the average length of time that product remains in inventory.

5. Account Receivable Turnover

= Sales/Accounts Receivable

Related financial ratio: Collection Period or Days Receivables = 365 × Accounts Receivable/Sales

This ratio measures the number of times that receivables turn over during the year. The higher the turnover of receivables, the shorter the time between sale and cash collection. If a company's Turnover Rate is significantly lower than industry norms, the underlying reason (poor collection methods, high risk customers, low sales) needs to be pinpointed.

The Days Receivables measures the average time in days that receivables are outstanding. The higher the number of days outstanding, the greater the collection risk. The days receivables rate may suggest a concern over credit control and collections.

6. Sales to Net Working Capital

= Sales/Net Working Capital

= Sales/(Current Assets − Current Liabilities)

Net Working capital levels higher than industry norms may indicate a strain on available liquid assets, while lower ratios may suggest too much liquidity—an inefficient use of capital. Working Capital is a concern of measure of current creditors since it reflects ability to finance current operations. Comparing sales from operations to working capital, indicates how well working capital is employed.

Exercises:

Below is Jim Corporation's Balance Sheet.

Jim Corporation

Balance Sheet

December 31, 2018

Assets	
Current Assets	
Cash on Deposit	$20,031
Accounts Receivable	$50,000
Inventory	$161,438
Total Current Assets	**$231,469**
Non-Current Assets	
Equipment	$152,324
Buildings	$165,237
Land	$83,470
Total Non-Current Assets	**$401,031**
Total Assets	**$632,500**
Liabilities	
Current Liabilities	
Accounts Payable	$142,168
Total Current Liabilities	**$142,168**
Non-Current Liabilities	
Equipment loan	$84,329
Real Estate Loan	$94,750
Total Non-Current Liabilities	**$179,079**
Total Liabilities	**$421,247**
Owners' Equity	
Common Stock	$280,000
Retained Earnings	$31,253
Total Owners' Equity	**$311,253**
Total Liabilities and Owners' Equity	**$632,500**

Additional information:

Sales are $500,000 and Cost of Goods Sold is $80,000.

The beginning inventory is $100,000.

Please analyze the financial statement of JIM Corporation according to the above financial ratios.

Unit 9　Income Statement

Study Objectives

After studying this unit, you should be able to:
- Define the major components of an income statement.
- Identify factors that can influence these components.
- Prepare an income statement.

Feature Story

Do you want to know about a company's profitability? Then make sure you know how to read EBITDA (Earnings Before Interest, Taxes, Depreciation, and Amortization) in an income statement. EBITDA is calculated as follows:

　　EBITDA = Revenues – Expenses (excluding tax, interest, depreciation and amortization)

EBITDA first came into common use in the 1980's, when it was used to indicate the ability of a company to pay back debts. As time passed, it became popular in industries with expensive assets that had to be written off over long periods of time. EBITDA is now commonly used by many companies, especially in the technology sector, even when it isn't warranted. EBITDA also leaves out the cash required for working capital and for the replacement of old equipment, which can be very costly. Consequently, EBITDA is often used in accounting to boost a company's earnings. In this case, is there any other index if we want to make sure that a company is not trying to hide something with EBITDA?

In this unit, all the elements in an income statement besides EBITDA are to be introduced. If you are a smart investor, you can never overlook them.

Unit 9 Income Statement

International Background Information

The Uses and Limitations of an Income Statement

The income statement provides investors and creditors with information that helps them predict the amounts, timing and uncertainty of future cash flows. Also, the income statement helps users determine the risk of not achieving particular cash flows.

The limitations of an income statement are:

◇ The statement does not include many items that contribute to general growth and well-being of an enterprise.

◇ Income figures are often affected by the accounting methods used.

◇ Income measures are subject to estimates.

9.1 Concept of the Income Statement

What Is an Income Statement?

Income statement, also known as profit and loss statement, is a summary of a company's profit or loss during any one given period of time, such as one month, three months, or one year. The income statement records all revenues for a business during this given period, as well as the operating expenses for the business. The income statement reveals a company's profitability, which reflects the company's performance and how much income can be reinvested into the company, or be passed onto investors in the form of dividends.

损益表

Income statement along with balance sheet, is the most basic element required by potential lenders, such as banks, investors, and vendors. They will use it to determine credit limits.

n. 供应商

What Is the Income Statement Used for?

The income statement is used for tracking revenues and expenses, by which you can determine the operating performance of your business over a period of time. Small business owners use it to find out what areas of their business are over budget or under budget. Specific items that are causing unexpected expenditures can be made clear, such as phone, fax, mail, or supply expenses. Meanwhile, income statement can track dramatic increases in product returns or in cost of goods sold as a percentage of sales, as well as be used to determine income tax liability.

9.2 Contents and Formats of the Income Statement

The income statement has been prepared traditionally in either single-step form or multiple-step form.

Single-Step Income Statement is to collect all revenues and all expenses separately, then subtract expenses from revenues, and educe the net income.

In Single-Step Form, a complete income statement has three sections—revenues, expenses and net income.

Below is the typical Single-Step Income Statement.

XYZ Company
Income Statement
December 31, 2018

Revenues	
Net Sales	$50,000
Interest Revenue	$3,000
Investment Revenue	$15,000
Total Revenues	**$68,000**
Expenses	
Cost of Goods Sold	$30,000
Selling Expenses	$5,000
Administrative Expenses	$3,200
Interest Expenses	$200
Income Taxes	$3,000
Total Expenses	**$41,400**
Net Income	**$26,600**

In the Multiple-Step Form, the content of income statement is divided into some items, which generate some interim information, and the net income can be computed through several steps. In order to understand the income statement, let's define the most essential items as they are listed.

- **Net Sales** are the total revenues generated from the sale of all the company's products or services minus "returns", "rebates" or "allowances".

- **Cost of Goods Sold** is what the company spent to make the things it sold. It includes the money the company spent to buy the raw materials needed to produce its products, and the money it spent on manufacturing its products and labor.

- **Operating Expenses** include marketing expenses, salaries, rent, and research and development costs. Any normal expense incurred in the day-to-day operations of the company is recorded under this category.

- **Other Income** means revenues that don't stem from the core operations of the business. This includes items such as capital gains (or losses) made from investments, foreign currency exchange, or income from the rental of properties, etc. Some of this income may be received regularly (e.g. from yearly dividends). They are still considered as other income, because they are outside main business activities.

- **Extraordinary Income** is often bulked together with other income, but it is better to be seen separately, because it represents profits or losses that do not occur on a regular, or even yearly basis. An example may be the expenses caused by a natural disaster.

- **Earnings before Interest and Tax (EBIT)** are the same as operating income, if a company does not have other and/or extraordinary income for a particular year. Any way, EBIT shows the investor a company's ability to pay interest expenses (such as on bonds or bank loans) with the income it has made for the year.

- **Interest Expenses** are the amount the company has to pay on debt owed. This could be assigned to bondholders or to banks. EBIT minus interest expenses equal earnings before tax.

- **Taxes** refer to income taxes, which all companies must pay. It is usually a percentage of income generated, and therefore will vary from year to year.

• **Net Profit after Taxes（NPAT）** is the money left over after all other duties have been paid. It is a key figure for shareholders, because it reveals the company's final income that can be distributed to shareholders and/or reinvested for future growth. 　税后净利润

• **Retained Earnings** are what's left after dividends are paid. This money is either used for future business ventures or invested back into the company for growth purposes. If a company pays dividends, it's considered to be income orientated. If it uses its NPAT for reinvestment into the company, it is considered growth orientated. Either way, it is important for an investor to understand a company's policies and goals to make sure that net earnings are being used in a satisfactory way. 　收益型　成长型

The income statement of XYZ Company for the year ended December 31, 2018, in the form of multiple-step is as follows.

XYZ Company

Income Statement

December 31, 2018

Net Sales	$50,000
Cost of Goods Sold	$30,000
Gross Profit	**$20,000**
Operating Expenses	
Selling Expenses	
Wages and Salaries	$2,200
Materials and Supplies	$500
Depreciation Expenses	$1,000
Total Selling Expenses	$3,700
Administrative Expenses	
Wages and Salaries	$2,800
Depreciation Expenses	$600
Other Administrative Expenses	$500
Total Administrative Expenses	$3,900
Total Operating Expenses	**$7,600**
Operating Income	**$12,400**
Other Revenues and Gains	
Rental Revenue	$200
Other Expenses and Losses	
Earnings before Interest and Tax	**$12,300**
Interest Expense	$300
Income Taxes	$4,920
Net Income	**$7,380**

The two forms have their advantages and disadvantages respectively. Single-step form is simple and perspicuous, while multiple-step form can provide more information, and users are able to know the different sources of the company's working achievements from its income statement. Correspondingly, this form is so difficult to understand that the users may be confused.

adj. 明白的，明了的

Notes

It is a key figure for shareholders, because it reveals the company's final income that can be distributed to shareholders and/or reinvested for future growth.
这是一个多重复合句。because 引导的原因状语从句中含有 that 引导的定语从句，修饰 income。该句的意思是：
对股东而言，税后净利润是一个关键数据，因为它揭示了可分配给股东或为未来增长进行再投资的企业最终收益。

9.3 How to Prepare the Income Statement

Whichever form is applied, an income statement should contain the following:

- **Title**

Income statement can also be called profit and loss statement, earnings statement, or statement of operations. Yet, income statement is the most popular term worldwide.

- **Heading**

Besides the name of the business and the name of the financial statement "Income Statement", the period involved and measuring unit employed should also be specified.

The preparing of income statement is based on the involved revenues and expenses ledgers. Different from the balance statement, the income statement is prepared according to the amounts occurred on revenues and expenses ledgers (accumulated amounts are included), while the balance statement is on the basis of the balance of assets, liabilities and owners' equity ledgers. Balance refers to the remaining sum of a particular date and the amounts occurred, however, represent the flow within an accounting period. In summary, the income statement bases on the formulae listed below.

Gross Profit = Net Sales – Cost of Goods Sold

Operating Income = Gross Profit - Total Operating Expenses

EBIT = Operating Income + (–) Other Income (Loss) + (–) Extraordinary Income (Loss)

Net Income = EBIT – Interest Expenses – Income Taxes

Retained Earnings = Net Income – Dividends

Below is the typical layout of an income statement. The concrete way to fill it in is as follows.

XYZ Company

Income Statement

December 31, 2018

Sales Revenue	The proceeds that come from sales to customers. Fill in the sheet upon the analysis of the amount occurred on the credit side of Sales ledger
Cost of Goods Sold	The expense that reflects the cost of the products or goods that generate revenue. Fill in the sheet upon the analysis of the amount occurred on the debt side of Cost of Goods Sold ledger
Gross Profit	Also called Gross Earnings, equals Sales Revenue minus Cost of Goods Sold
Operating Expenses	Any expense that doesn't fit under Cost of Goods Sold. Fill in the sheet upon the analysis of the amount occurred on the debt side of such as administrative, marketing expenses ledger and so on
Earnings before Interest and Tax	Net income before taking interest and income tax expenses into account
Interest Expenses	The payments made on the company's outstanding debt. Fill in the sheet upon the analysis of the amount occurred on the debt side of Interest Expenses ledger
Income Taxes	The amount payable to the government. Fill in the sheet upon the analysis of the amount occurred on the debt side of Income Taxes ledger
Net Income	The final profit after deducting all expenses from all revenues

Unit 9 Income Statement

Notes

Besides the name of the business and the name of the financial statement "Income Sheet", the period involved and measuring unit employed should also be specified.

besides 意为"除了……之外还"，相当于 in addition to；过去分词 involved 后置修饰 period，译为所涵盖的期间；同样过去分词 employed 后置修饰 measuring unit，译为所采用的计量单位。该句的意思是：

除了企业名称和报表名称"利润表"外，还要明确表明报表所涵盖的期间及所采用的计量单位。

Assignment

Ⅰ. **Select the best answer for each of the following questions or uncompleted sentences.**

（1） **Which financial statement illustrates the financial results of a company's operations and provides a "financial accounting bridge" between a company's prior and current period balance sheets? _____.**

　　A. The cash flow statement

　　B. The statement of retained income

　　C. The income statement

　　D. No one statement can properly illustrate the financial results of a company's operations

（2） **The major elements of the income statement are _____.**

　　A. revenue, cost of goods sold, selling expenses, and general expense

　　B. operating section, nonoperating section, discontinued operations, extraordinary items, and cumulative effect

　　C. revenues, expenses, gains and losses

　　D. all of these

（3） **Information in the income statement helps users to _____.**

　　A. evaluate the past performance of the enterprise

　　B. provide a basis for predicting future performance

　　C. help assess the risk or uncertainty of achieving future cash flows

　　D. all of these

（4） **Limitations of the income statement include all of the following except _____.**

　　A. items that cannot be measured reliably are not reported

　　B. only actual amounts are reported in determining net income

　　C. income measurement involves judgment

　　D. income numbers are affected by the accounting methods employed

(5) Classification as an extraordinary item on the income statement would be appropriate for the _____.

    A. gain or loss on disposal of a segment of the business

    B. substantial write-off of obsolete inventories

    C. loss from a strike

    D. none of these

(6) Which of these is generally an example of an extraordinary item?_____.

    A. Loss incurred because of a strike by employees

    B. Write-off of deferred marketing costs believed to have no future benefit

    C. Gain resulting from the devaluation of the U. S. dollar

    D. Gain resulting from the state exercising its right of eminent domain on a piece of land used as a parking lot

(7) During its first year, a corporation had revenues of $200,000 and also had the following changes: ① assets increased by $40,000; ② liabilities decreased by $20,000; ③ paid-in capital increased by $50,000. What are the corporation's expenses for the year? _____.

    A. $190,000   B. $230,000

    C. $270,000   D. $310,000

(8) A corporation's retained income increased $240,000 during the past year. Cash dividends declared during the year totaled $60,000, and the revenues were twice the expenses. What is the dollar amount of the revenues? _____.

    A. $120,000   B. $150,000

    C. $200,000   D. $600,000

(9) Which of the following is an example of a ratio? _____.

    A. $9,000 + 40,000$ B. $9,000 \times 40,000$

    C. $9,000/40,000$ D. $\sqrt{9,000}$

(10) Which one of the following statements best describes the accounting effects of a cash dividend declaration? _____.

    A. Liabilities are increased and stockholders' equity is decreased

    B. Assets and stockholders' equity are both decreased

    C. Assets and liabilities are both decreased

    D. Liabilities and stockholders' equity are both decreased

II. Case Analysis

During the year 2018, ABC company took place the items as follows:

(1) Receipted net sales for $450,000, while the cost of goods sold is $350,000.

(2) Receipted the rental revenue for $3,500.

(3) Paid all wages and salaries for $18,000, among them $10,000 belonging to the sellers and $8,000 for the managers.
(4) Paid the business entertainment expenses $5,000, among them $4,000 belonging to the sales department, the rest belonging to the management section.
(5) Paid $2,400 business traveling expenses for sales department, and $1,200 for office expenses.
(6) Expended $4,500 to pay for the short-term loan interest.
(7) All depreciation expenses were $11,000.
(8) The loss of fixed assets found in a fixed asset count was $6,200.
(9) Paid income taxes for $8,500.

Please fill in the blanks to help ABC Company preparing for a Multiple-step Income Statement.

ABC Company
Income Statement
December 31, 2018

Net Sales	(	)
Cost of Goods Sold	(	)
Gross Profit	(	)
Operating Expenses		
Selling Expenses		
Wages and Salaries	(	)
Entertainment Expenses	(	)
Traveling Expenses	(	)
Administrative Expenses		
Wages and Salaries	(	)
Entertainment Expenses	(	)
Traveling Expenses	(	)
Depreciation Expenses	(	)
Total Operating Expenses	(	)
Operating Income	(	)
Other Revenues and Gains		
Rental Revenue	(	)
Other Expenses and Losses		
Loss on Disposal of Equipment	(	)
Earnings before Interest and Tax	(	)
Interest Expenses	(	)
Income Taxes	(	)
Net Income	(	)

Reading Material

Income Statement Analysis

The income statement is a basic record for reporting a company's earnings. Since earnings are a fundamental component in a firm's worth, it is essential for investors to know how to analyze different elements of this important document.

This section is designed to teach you some basic methods for analyzing the income statement. Analyzing income statements is an important tool to help investors appraise their investment options. By analyzing an income statement properly, investors can begin to evaluate the effectiveness of the management of operations in the companies in which they are interested in investing. Proper income statement analysis can help identify good investment opportunities. It can also reduce the risk involved with choosing a poor investment choice.

Interest Coverage is the measurement of how many times interest payments could be made with a firm's earnings before interest expenses and taxes are paid. From a bondholder's perspective, interest coverage is a test to see whether a firm could have problems making their interest payments. From an equity holder's perspective, this ratio helps to give some indication of the short-term financial health of the company.

The following formula is used to determine the coverage of interest:

Interest Coverage Ratio = Earnings before Interest and Tax (EBIT) /Interest Expenses

A higher ratio is typically better for bondholders and equity investors. For bondholders a high ratio indicates a low probability that the firm will go bankrupt in the near term. A company with a high interest coverage ratio can meet their interest obligations several times over. Stock investors typically like companies with high interest coverage ratio, too. A high ratio indicates a company that is probably relatively solvent. Thus, all other things equal, an investor should be very careful with firms that have a low interest coverage ratio with respect to other companies in their industry.

Since the fundamental purpose of the income statement is to report profits or losses, understanding the various profitability ratios that follow is extremely helpful to your analysis of a firm.

Profitability is often measured in percentage terms in order to facilitate making comparisons of a company's financial performance against past year's performance and against the performance of other companies.

When profitability is expressed as a percentage (or ratio), the new figures are called profit margins. The most common profit margins are all expressed as percentages of Net Sales.

Let's look at a few of the most commonly used profit margins that you can easily learn to use to help you measure and compare firms:

Gross Margin is the resulting percentage when Gross Profit is divided by Net Sales. Remember that Gross Profit is equal to Net Sales minus Cost of Goods Sold. Therefore, Gross Margin represents the percentage of revenue remaining after Cost of Goods Sold is deducted.

Gross Margin = Gross Profit/Net Sales

Since this ratio only takes into account sales and variable costs (costs of goods sold), this ratio is a good indicator of a firm's efficiency in producing and distributing its products. A firm with a ratio superior to the industry average demonstrates superior efficiency in its production processes. The higher the ratio, the higher the efficiency of the production process. Investors tend to favor companies that are more efficient.

Operating Margin is the resulting ratio when Operating Income is divided by Net Sales.

Operating Margin = Operating Income/Net Sales

This ratio measures the quality of a firm's operations. A firm with a high operating margin in relation to the industry average has operations that are more efficient. Typically, to achieve this result, the company must have lower fixed costs, a better gross margin, or a combination of the two. At any rate, companies that are more efficient than their competitors in their core operations have a distinct advantage. Most investors will tend to prefer a more efficient company.

Net Margin is a measure of profitability for the sum of a firm's operations. It is equal to Net Income divided by Net Sales.

Net Margin = Net Income/Net Sales

As with the other ratios you will want to compare Net Margin with other companies in the industry. You can also track year-to-year changes in Net Margin to see if a company's competitive position is improving, or getting worse.

The higher the Net Margin relative to the industry (or relative to past years), the better. However, as with all the previous Profit Margin measurements, you need to always check past years of performance. You must make sure that good results are not a "fluke". Strong Profit Margin that is sustainable, indicates that a company has been able to consistently outperform their competitors. The savvy investor uses profitability margins to help analyze income statements of prospective investments. Companies with high Interest Coverage Ratio, Gross Margin, Operating Margin and Net Margin will always be very attractive to investors.

Exercises:

Please compute the following financial ratio for ABC Company: Interest Coverage Ratio, Gross Margin, Operating Margin, and Net Margin.

Unit 10
Statement of Cash Flows

Study Objectives

After studying this unit, you should be able to:
- Define cash and cash equivalents.
- Understand and identify operating activities, investing activities, financing activities.
- Understand the direct method and the indirect method when you prepare a statement of cash flows.
- Prepare a statement of cash flows.

Feature Story

Catherine's business is growing, and she's making a good profit. However, she never seems to have enough money to pay her bills. This month she had to pay the business insurance premium with her credit card.

Catherine has what is known as a "cash flow problem". It means that the cash flowing into her business is out of synch with the cash moving out. The result is that she is temporarily caught short when her bills come due. Catherine needs to plan ahead so she will know whether or not she will have enough cash available when she needs it.

How many of you have had something similar happen to you? Business analysts report that poor management is the major reason why most businesses fail. It would probably be more accurate to say that business failure is due to poor cash management. So how can you manage your cash situation better?

In this unit, we'll take a look at the cash flow process, and find out how to prepare statement of cash flows.

Unit 10　Statement of Cash Flows

International Background Information

Purpose of the Statement of Cash Flows

As indicated earlier, the balance sheet and the income statement present, to a limited extent, information about the cash flows of an enterprise during a period. For instance, comparative balance sheets might show what new assets have been acquired or disposed of and what liabilities have been incurred or liquidated. The income statement provides information about resources, but not exactly cash, resulted from operations.

In other words, neither the balance sheet nor income statement presents a detailed summary of all the cash inflows and outflows, or the sources and uses of cash during the period. To fill this need, the FASB requires the statement of cash flows (also called the cash flow statement).

The primary purpose of a statement of cash flows is to provide relevant information about the cash receipts and cash payments of an enterprise during a given period.

To achieve this purpose, the statement of cash flows reports: ①the cash effects of operations during the given period; ②investing transactions; ③financing transactions; ④the net increase or decrease in cash during the period.

现金流量

vt. 清偿

现金流量表

Notes

The primary purpose of a statement of cash flows is to provide relevant information about the cash receipts and cash payments of an enterprise during a given period.
现金流量表的基本目的是提供企业在一定期间内的现金收支情况。

10.1　Concept of the Statement of Cash Flows

The statement of cash flows is used to analyze the inflows and outflows of cash and cash equivalents during a designated time period. At present, the statement of cash flows uses generalized "cash" as the foundation of preparing.

现金等价物

What Is Cash?

The statement of cash flows is concerned only with cash and cash equivalents, which include cash on hand, cash in the bank, and any cash invested in what is defined as short-term, highly liquid financial instruments. Generally, only instruments with original maturities of three months or less are cash equivalents. Accepted cash equivalents include treasury bills, commercial paper, and money market funds. These might be converted to cash at some point in time. Profit growth does not necessarily mean more cash as we will see.

What Are Cash Flows?

Cash flows simply refer to the flows of cash into and out of a business over a period of time. Watching cash inflows and outflows is one of the major management tasks of an owner. The outflows of cash are measured by those checks you write every month to pay salaries, suppliers, and creditors. The inflows are the cash you receive from customers, lenders and investors.

There are certain items which may not affect your income statement for some time, such as:

- Substantial increase in inventory purchases.
- Increase in accounts receivable.
- Reduction of credit by suppliers.
- Purchase of equipment.
- Unrecognized obsolescence of inventory (stale items).
- Bank's refusal to renew or extend loan.
- Lump-sum payment of debts.

The statement of cash flows will highlight these activities in a way that an income statement will not.

Who Cares about the Statement of Cash Flows?

Executives want to know if the cash generated by the company is sufficient to fund their expansion strategy.

Stockholders want to know if the firm is generating enough

cash to pay dividends.

Suppliers want to know if their customers are able to pay for offered credit.

Investors want to evaluate future growth potential.

Employees are interested in the overall viability of their employers to fund their operations.

n. 生存能力

Certainly, the banks also want to see the statement of cash flows showing how the company has used the funds from a previous loan before they approve an extension or a new one.

Notes

Certainly, the banks also want to see the statement of cash flows showing how the company has used the funds from a previous loan before they approve an extension or a new one.
这是一个含有由 before 引导的时间状语从句的复合句。主句中有 how 引导的宾语从句。该句的意思是：
当然银行也想在同意给贷款延期或重新贷款前，通过现金流量表来了解企业是如何使用前期的贷款资金的。

10.2　Contents and Formats of the Statement of Cash Flows

The statement of cash flows is divided into three sections including internal and external sources as follows:
- Cash flows from operating activities（Internal）.
- Cash flows from investing activities（Internal）.
- Cash flows from financing activities（External）.

International Insight

International Accounting Standard 7 requires a statement of cash flows. Both international standards and U. S. GAAP specify that the cash flows must be classified as operating, investing, or financing.

Cash Flows from Operating Activities

Operating activities usually involve producing and delivering goods and providing services. Cash flows from Operating activities, often referred to as working capital, are the cash flows generated from internal operations. They are the cash flows generated from sales of the products or services of your business. They are the real lifeblood of your business, and because they are generated internally, they are under your control.

Cash receipts include:
- Sale of goods or services.
- Interest revenue.
- Dividend revenue.

Cash payments include:
- Inventory purchases.
- Payroll.
- Taxes and Interest expenses.
- Others (utilities, rent, etc.).

Cash Flows from Investing Activities

Investing activities include transactions and events involving the purchase and sale of securities (excluding cash equivalents), land, buildings, equipment, and other assets not generally held for resale, and also cover the making and collecting of loans. Investing activities are classified not in the same way as operating activities, because they have an indirect relationship to the central, ongoing operation of your business (usually the sale of goods or services).

Cash receipts include:
- Sale of property, plant and equipment.
- Sale of a business segment.
- Sale of investments in equity securities of other entities or debt securities (other than cash equivalents).
- Collection of principal on loans made to other entities.

Cash payments include:
- Purchase of property, plant and equipment.
- Purchase of equity securities of other entities or debt securities (other than cash equivalents).
- Loans to other entities.

营运资本

n. 生命必需的血液，活力的源泉

n. 薪水册，薪金总额，应付工资总数

n. 有价证券

n. 分割的部分
（股票等）权益证券
（债券等）债务证券

Cash Flows from Financing Activities

All financing activities deal with the flows of cash to or from the business owners (equity financing) and creditors (debt financing). For example, cash proceeds from issuing capital stock or bonds would be classified under financing activities. Likewise, payments to repurchase stock (treasury stock) or to retire bonds and the payment of dividends are financing activities as well.

Cash receipts include:
- Issuance of own stock.
- Borrowing (bonds, notes, mortgages, etc.).

Cash payments include:
- Dividends to stockholders.
- Repaying principal amounts borrowed.
- Repurchasing business' own stock (treasury stock).

10.3 How to Prepare the Statement of Cash Flows

The following is the basic format for a statement of cash flows.

Statement of Cash Flows	
Cash Flows from Operating Activities	$×××
Cash Flows from Investing Activities	$×××
Cash Flows from Financing Activities	$×××
Net Increase (Decrease) in Cash	$×××
Cash at Beginning of Year	$×××
Cash at End of Year	$×××

Cash flows arising from the operating activities of the business are cash inflows and outflows directly related to the items of income statement. However, the income statement can't reflect the cash flows in the operating activities, because it is based on the accrual basis. Therefore, it is necessary to replace the accrual basis with the cash basis. There are two methods for the replacement—indirect method and direct method. Although both of them produce identical results, the indirect method is used more often because it reconciles the difference between the net income and the net cash flows provided by operations.[1]

International Insight

Statements of cash flows are not required in all countries. Some nations require a statement reporting sources and applications of "funds" (often defined as working capital). Others have no requirement for either cash or funds flow statements.

Indirect Method

Indirect method is popular because of its relative simplicity. This method starts with a figure for the net income (from your income statement), and helps you adjust from this accrual basis to the cash basis for any items that do not affect cash flows.[2] Below is the formula.

Cash Flows from Operating Activities

= Net Income (Note: take directly from income statement)

+ Expenses and Losses that not involve cash inflows or outflows

+ Decreases in Current Assets or Increases in Current Liabilities

− Revenues and Gains that not involve cash inflows or outflows

− Increases in Current Assets or Decreases in Current Liabilities (Note: Increases in current assets do not include cash or cash equivalents when determining this item.)

Sample of Statement of Cash Flows under Indirect Method is as follow.

ABC Company

Statement of Cash Flows

December 31, 2018

Cash Flows from Operating Activities	
Net Income①	$207,901
Additions (Sources of Cash)	

		（续）
	Depreciation	$130,900
	Increase in Accounts Payable	$12,034
	Increase in Accrued Income Taxes	$41,500
Subtractions（Uses of Cash）		
	Increase in Accounts Receivable	$111,800
	Increase in Inventory	-$95,300
Net Cash Flows from Operating Activities		**$375,835**
Cash Flows from Investing Activities		
	Equipment	-$104,200
Net Cash Flows from Investing Activities		**-$104,200**
Cash Flows from Financing Activities		
	Notes Payable	$400,000
Net Cash Flows from Financing Activities		**$400,000**
Net Change in Cash		**$671,635**

① Net Income is taken directly from income statement.

n. 减少

Direct Method

Instead of starting with a reported net income, the direct method analyzes the various types of operating activities and calculates the total cash flows created by each one. Before beginning the direct method, all accrual accounts must first be converted to a cash figure.

This sample of worksheet helps explain how the amounts are determined in the statement of cash flows under direct method.

A.	**Cash Receipts from Customers**	
	Net Sales	$×××
	Add: Beginning Accounts Receivable	$×××
	Less: Ending Accounts Receivable	$×××
	Cash Receipts from Customers	$×××
B.	**Cash Payments for Inventory**	
	Add: Ending Inventory	$×××
	Less: Beginning Inventory	$×××
	Add: Beginning Accounts Payable	$×××
	Less: Ending Accounts Payable	$×××
	Cash Paid for Inventory	$×××

(续)

C.	**Cash Paid for Operating Expenses**	
	Operating Expenses	$×××
	Less: Depreciation Expenses	$×××
	Add: Ending Prepaid Expenses	$×××
	Less: Beginning Prepaid Expenses	$×××
	Add: Beginning Expenses Payable	$×××
	Less: Ending Expenses Payable	$×××
	Cash Paid for Operating Expenses	$×××
D.	**Cash Paid for Interest Expenses**	
	Interest Expenses	$×××
	Add: Beginning Interest Payable	$×××
	Less: Ending Interest Payable	$×××
	Cash Paid for Interest Expenses	$×××
E.	**Cash Paid for Corporate Income Taxes**	
	Income Taxes	$×××
	Add: Beginning Taxes Payable	$×××
	Less: Ending Taxes Payable	$×××
	Cash Paid for Corporate Income Taxes	$×××

Below is the sample of Statement of Cash Flows under Direct Method.

XYZ Company
Statement of Cash Flows
December 31, 2018

Cash Flows from Operating Activities	
Cash Receipts from Customers	$1,342,500
Cash Paid for Inventory	$392,266
Cash Paid for Operating Expenses	$300,000
Cash Paid for Interest Expenses	$70,000
Cash Paid for Corporate Income Taxes	$204,399
Net Cash Flows from Operating Activities	**$375,835**
Cash Flows from Investing Activities	
Proceeds from Sale of Equipment	$346,800
Purchase of Equipment	$451,000
Net Cash Flows from Investing Activities	**−$104,200**
Cash Flows from Financing Activities	
Long-Term Borrowings	$400,000
Reduction of Long-Term Debts	$1,282,500
Net Cash Flows from Financing Activities	**−$882,500**
Net Increase (Decrease) in Cash	**−$610,865**

Notes

1. Although both of them produce identical results, the indirect method is used more often because it reconciles the difference between the net income and the net cash flows provided by operations.

   这是含有 although 引导的让步状语从句的复合句。在主句中还有一个 because 引导的原因状语从句。该句的意思是：

   虽然两者产生的结果是一样的，但是间接法更常用一些，这是因为它调和了由经营活动提供的净收益和净现金流量之间的差别。

2. This method starts with a figure for the net income (from your income statement), and helps you adjust from this accrual basis to the cash basis for any items that do not affect cash flows.

   该句的意思是：间接法从净利润（来自于利润表）开始帮你将那些不影响现金流的项目从权责发生制调整到现金收付制上来。

Assignment

Ⅰ. Select the best answer for each of the following questions or uncompleted sentences.

(1) The statement of cash flows classifies cash receipts and cash payments by the following activities: _____.

   A. operating and nonoperating
   B. investing, financing, and operating
   C. financing, operating, and nonoperating
   D. investing, financing, and nonoperating

(2) An example of a cash flow from an operating activity is _____.

   A. payment of cash to lenders for interest
   B. receipt of cash from the sale of capital stock
   C. payment of cash dividends to the company's stockholders
   D. none of the above

(3) Cash dividends paid to stockholders are classified on the statement of cash flows as _____.

   A. operating activities   B. investing activities
   C. financing activities   D. a combination of the above

(4) An example of a cash flow from an investing activity is _____.

   A. receipt of cash from the issuance of bonds payable
   B. payment of cash to repurchase outstanding capital stock
   C. receipt of cash from the sale of equipment
   D. payment of cash to suppliers for inventory

(5) An example of a cash flow from a financing activity is _____.

A. payment of cash to lenders for interest

B. receipt of cash from the sale of land

C. issuance of debt for cash

D. purchase of equipment for cash

II. Mark the correct items by "√" and the wrong items by " × ".

(1) Accounting is a system of providing quantitative informatin, primarily fianancial in nature, about economic entities that is intended to be useful in making economic decisions. (   )

(2) Financial accounting is the name given to accounting systems designed for internal users. (   )

(3) The primary financial statements are the profit and loss account, balance sheet, and income tax return. (   )

(4) A company's financial statements are useful to potential lenders, because they help judge whether the company wil be able to repay a loan. (   )

(5) A company's suppliers have no use for the company's financial statements, because they only sell the products to the company, and do not invest in it or lend to it. (   )

III. Study the brief case and finish the exercise.

Eddie Company reported a net income of $195,000 for 2018. Eddie also reported a depreciation expense of $35,000, and a loss of $5,000 on the sale of equipment. The company sheets show an increase in accounts receivable of $15,000 for the year, and $8,000 in accounts payable, and a decrease in prepaid expenses of $4,000. Cash flows from operating activities of Eddie Company for 2018 are $_____.

IV. Case Analysis

The income statement of William Company is shown below.

William Company
Income Statement
December 31, 2018

Net Sales	**$7,100,000**
Cost of Goods Sold	
Beginning Inventory	$1,700,000
Purchases	$5,430,000
Goods Available for Sale	$7,130,000
Ending Inventory	$1,920,000
Total Cost of Goods Sold	**$5,210,000**
Gross Profit	**$1,890,000**

（续）

Operating Expenses	
Selling Expenses	$380,000
Administrative Expenses	$525,000
Depreciation Expenses	$75,000
Amortization Expenses	$30,000
Total Operating Expenses	**$1,010,000**
Net Income	**$880,000**

Additional information:

(1) Accounts receivable increased $490,000 during the year.

(2) Prepaid expenses increased $170,000 during the year.

(3) Accounts payable to merchandise suppliers increased $40,000 during the year.

(4) Accrued expenses payable decreased $180,000 during the year.

Please prepare the operating activities section of the statement of cash flows for the year ended December 31, 2018 for William Company by using the indirect method.

Reading Material

Analyzing the Statement of Cash Flows

Let's take a look at the sample of a statement of cash flows.

XYZ Company

Statement of Cash Flows

December 31, 2018

Cash Flows from Operating Activities	
Net Income	$2,000,000
Addition to Cash	
Depreciation	$10,000
Decrease in Accounts Receivable	$15,000
Increase in Taxes Payable	$2,000
Subtraction from Cash	
Decrease in Accounts Payable	$15,000
Increase in Inventory	$30,000
Net Cash from Operating Activities	**$1,982,000**

（续）

Cash Flows from Investing Activities	
Equipment	−$500,000
Net Cash from Investing Activities	**−$500,000**
Cash Flows from Financing Activities	
Notes Payable	$10,000
Net Cash from Financing Activities	**$10,000**
Cash Flows from FY Ended 31 Dec 2018	**$1,492,000**

From this statement of cash flows, we can see that the cash flow for fiscal year 2018 is $1,492,000. The bulk of the positive cash flow stems from cash earned from operations, which is a good sign for investors. It means that core operations are generating business and that there is enough money to buy new inventory. The purchasing of new equipment shows that the company has cash to invest in inventory for growth. Finally, the amount of cash available to the company should ease investors' minds regarding the notes payable, as cash is plentiful to cover that future loan expense.

Of course, not all statements of cash flows look this healthy, presenting a positive cash flow. But a negative cash flow should not automatically raise a red light without some further analysis. Sometimes, a negative cash flow is a result of a company's decision to expand its business at a certain point in time, which, in fact, would be a good thing for the future. This is why analyzing changes in cash flow from one period to the next gives the investor a better idea of how the company is performing, and whether or not a company may be on the brink of bankruptcy or success.

The statement of cash flows is derived from the income statement and the balance sheet. Net earnings from the income statement is the figure from which the information on the statement of cash flows is deduced. As for the balance sheet, the net cash flow in the statement of cash flows from one year to the next should equal the increase or decrease of cash between the two consecutive balance sheets that apply to the period that the statement of cash flows covers.

A company can use the statement of cash flows to predict future cash flows, which helps with matters in budgeting. For investors, the cash flows reflect a company's financial health: basically, the more cash available for business operations, the better. However, this is not a hard and fast rule. Sometimes a negative cash flow results from a company's growth strategy in the form of expanding its operations.

By adjusting earnings, revenues, assets and liabilities, the investor can get a very clear picture of the most important aspect of a company: how much cash it generates and, particularly, how much of that cash stems from core operations.

APPENDIX

Appendix Ⅰ

参考答案

Unit 1
Assignment

Ⅰ. (1) D (2) D (3) A (4) B (5) C (6) B (7) B (8) D
Ⅱ. (1) × (2) × (3) × (4) √ (5) √ (6) √

Reading Material

(1) d (2) j (3) f (4) h (5) g (6) i (7) e (8) c (9) a (10) b

Unit 2
Assignment

Ⅰ. (1) D (2) A (3) A (4) D (5) A (6) B (7) B (8) E (9) C (10) B
Ⅱ. (1) × (2) × (3) × (4) × (5) √ (6) √ (7) × (8) √ (9) √ (10) √
Ⅲ.

May 1: Cash increases $8,000 with a debit. Capital Stock increases $8,000 with a credit.

Cash	$8,000
Capital Stock	$8,000

May 2: Cash decreases $2,500 with a credit. Tools & Equipment increase $2,500 with a debit.

Property, Plant and Equipment	$2,500
(Tools & Equipment)	
Cash	$2,500

May 8: Vehicles increase $15,000 with a debit. Cash decreases $2,000 with a credit. Notes Payable increases $13,000 with a credit.

Property, Plant and Equipment	$15,000
Vehicles	
Cash	$2,000
Notes Payable	$13,000

May 18: Tools & Equipment decrease $150 with a credit. Accounts Receivable increase $150 with a debit.

  Accounts Receivable $150
   Property, Plant and Equipment $150
   (Tools & Equipment)

May 29: Cash increases $750 with a debit. Sales Revenue increases $750 with a credit.

  Cash $750
   Sales Revenue $750

May 31: Cash decreases $50 with a credit. Operating Expense increases $50 with a debit.

  Operating Expense $50
   Cash $50

Now, let's look at the trial balance for BHK Company for the month of May.

Operating Expense		Sales Revenue		Accounts Receivable	
5/31 50			5/29 750	5/18 150	

Capital Stock		Notes Payable	
	5/1 8,000		5/8 13,000

Cash	
5/1 8,000	5/2 2,500
5/29 750	5/8 2,000
	5/31 50

Property, Plant and Equipment	
5/2 2,500	5/18 150
5/8 15,000	

BHK Company
Trial Balance
May 31, 20××

Cash	$	4,200
Accounts Receivable	$	150
Property, Plant and Equipment	$	17,350
Notes Payable		$ 13,000
Capital Stock		$ 8,000
Sales Revenue		$ 750
Operating Expense	$	50
Total	$ 21,750	$ 21,750

Reading Material

(1) Bookkeeping is a mechanical process that records the routine economic activities of a business. Accounting includes bookkeeping but goes beyond it in scope.

(2) An accountant designs accounting systems, analyzes and interprets financial information, prepares financial statements, conducts audits, makes forecasts and budgets, and provides tax services.

Unit 3
Assignment

Ⅰ. (1) C   (2) D   (3) C   (4) B   (5) D   (6) A   (7) B   (8) A   (9) C   (10) D

APPENDIX

II. (1) ×　(2) √　(3) √　(4) ×　(5) √

III. (1) $690　(2) $470

IV.

Item one: goods held on consignment for Fred Co., are the assets of that company and should not be regarded as inventories of Hargrove Company. So 15,000 units should be subtracted from the total inventory.

Item two: purchased goods in transit on term of FOB can be recognized as the company's assets and included in the inventory.

Item three: Sold inventory in transit on term of FOB should not be considered as the Hargrove Company's assets nor included in the inventory.

The quantity of inventory of Hargrove Company should be 195,000 units (200,000 – 15,000 + 10,000).

Reading Material (Omitted)

Unit 4

Assignment

I. (1) C　(2) A　(3) C　(4) D　(5) A　(6) D　(7) C　(8) D　(9) A　(10) B

II. (1) $18,300 (= $18,000 + $200 + $100)

(2) ① $28,000 (= $30,000 – $2,000)　② $2,000 (= $28,000/14)

(3) ① $40,000 (= $44,000 – $4,000)　② $0.4 (= $40,000/100,000)

　　③ $6,000 (= $0.4 × 15,000)

(4) ① $30,000　② $40,000　③ $2,000

III. ① The cost of this plant asset is $25,900 (= $22,000 + $1,300 + $600 + $200 + $1,000 + $800).

② The depreciation for each of the first two years by the straight-line method: the first year is $2,590 and the second year is $2,590.

③ The depreciation for each of the first two years by the unit-of-production method: the first year is $49.21 and the second year is $6,475.

Reading Material

(1) F　(2) F　(3) F　(4) T　(5) T

Unit 5

Assignment

I. (1) A　(2) D　(3) A　(4) B　(5) B

II. (1) √　(2) √　(3) ×　(4) ×　(5) √

III. (1) Cash ＄100,000, Bonds payable ＄100,000

(2) non-current, current

(3) all assets

(4) probable, can

(5) ＄665

IV. Analysis: In this case, G. Company has essentially purchased the equipment and this lease should be referred to as a capital lease (refer to the text). First, the lease term is 80% (more than 75%) of the economic life of the asset. Second, the present value of cash payments is equal to fair market value. The entry is as follows:

Leased Asset—Equipment   ＄190,000

    Lease Liability   ＄190,000

Reading Material (Omitted)

Unit 6

Assignment

I. (1) A, B   (2) B   (3) B   (4) C, C, B   (5) A   (6) A

II. (1) √   (2) ×   (3) √   (4) √   (5) ×

III. (1) increases, ￥110,000 (= ￥100,000 – ￥20,000 + ￥30,000)

(2) ￥500,000, Retained earnings ￥500,000, Cash ￥500,000, increased, unchanged, decreased

(3) 20% (￥1.10 divided by ￥5.50)

IV. Suggested solution:

(1) Henry Ford decided to set his firm a mass-production. To achieve this aim would require large factories and many workers, which meant a large sum of money. The most swift and efficient way to raise the funds was to issue stock.

(2) Ford Motor Company issued a massive treasury stock purchase when Henry Ford's didn't hold the identical wishes with the ones of the shareholders.

(3) The history of Ford Motor Company illustrates lots of strengths and weakness of forming a corporation. There are many efficient ways of raising funds to form a corporation and expand the firm. However, by issuing shares, Henry Ford relinquished control over the firm. This led to a collision in 1916 when he believed that it was in the firm's best interest to retain funds rather than to pay dividends. As the outside shareholders were not as well-treated as a corporation's managers, the shareholders may force management to do things which hindered the firm's success.

Reading Material

(1) F   (2) T   (3) F   (4) F   (5) T

Unit 7

Assignment

Ⅰ. (1) B (2) E (3) D (4) C (5) E (6) B
Ⅱ. (1) √ (2) × (3) √ (4) √ (5) × (6) √
Ⅲ.

    Administrative expenses increase $27,000 in all.

    Financial expenses increase $7,800 in all.

    Selling expenses increase $83,600 in all.

    Non-operating expenses increase $6,200 in all.

    Net investment profit decreases $2,500 in all.

Reading Material

(1) T (2) T (3) F (4) F (5) F

Unit 8

Assignment

Ⅰ. (1) C (2) C (3) D (4) A (5) B
Ⅱ.

ABC Company

Balance Sheet

December 31, 2018

Assets	
Cash	$247,485
Accounts Receivable	$649,024
Merchandise Inventory	$189,713
Property, Plant and Equipment	$1,125,800
Less: Accumulated Depreciation	$325,200
Total Assets	**$1,886,822**
Liabilities and Owners' Equity	
Accounts Payable	$229,530
Notes Payable	$13,000
Wages Payable	
Income Taxes Payable	$500
Bonds Payable	$500,000
Total Liabilities	**$743,030**
Owners' Equity	
Common Stock	$600,000

	（续）
Retained Earnings	$543,792
Total Owners' Equity	**$1,143,792**
Total Liabilities and Owners' Equity	**$1,886,822**

Reading Material

（1）Quick Ratio = 0.49

（2）Current Ratio = 1.63

（3）Current Assets to Cash = 11.56

（4）Inventory Turnover = 0.61

　　Days in Inventory = 730

（5）Accounts Receivable Turnover = 10

　　Or Days Receivables = 36.5

（6）Sales to Net Working Capital = 5.60

Unit 9
Assignment

Ⅰ.（1）C　（2）C　（3）D　（4）D　（5）D　（6）D　（7）A　（8）D　（9）C　（10）A

Ⅱ.

ABC Company Income Statement

December 31, 2018

Net Sales	($450,000)
Cost of Goods Sold	($350,000)
Gross Profit on Sales	($100,000)
Operating Expenses	
Selling Expenses	
Wages and Salaries	($10,000)
Entertainment Expenses	($4,000)
Traveling Expenses	($2,400)
Administrative Expenses	
Wages and Salaries	($8,000)
Entertainment Expenses	($1,000)
Traveling Expenses	($1,200)
Depreciation Expenses	($11,000)
Total Operating Expenses	($37,600)
Operating Income	($62,400)

（续）

Other Revenues and Gains	
Rental Revenue	($3,500)
Other Expenses and Losses	
Loss on Disposal of Equipment	($6,200)
Earnings before Interest and Tax	($59,700)
Interest Expenses	($4,500)
Income Taxes	($8,500)
Net Income	($46,700)

Reading Material

Interest Coverage Ratio = 13.27

Gross Margin = 22.22%

Operating Margin = 13.87%

Net Margin = 10.38%

Unit 10

Assignment

I. (1) B　(2) A　(3) D　(4) C　(5) C

II. (1) √　(2) ×　(3) ×　(4) √　(5) ×

III. $232,000　(232,000 = 195,000 + 35,000 + 5,000 − 15,000 + 8,000 + 4,000)

IV. Net cash flows from operating activities are −$35,000.

William Company

Statement of Cash Flows

December 31, 2018

Cash Flows from Operating Activities	
Net Income	$880,000
Additions (Sources of Cash)	
Depreciation	$75,000
Amortization	$30,000
Increase in Accounts Payable	$40,000
Subtractions (Uses of Cash)	
Increase in Prepaid Expenses	$170,000
Increase in Accounts Receivable	$490,000
Increase in Inventory	$220,000
Decrease in Expenses Payable	$180,000
Net Cash Flows from Operating Activities	**−$35,000**

Reading Material

(Omitted)

Appendix Ⅱ

课文参考译文

第一单元　会计总论

1.1　会计的产生与发展

会计学的重要性

今天，许多人以从事会计职业而自豪。事实上，几乎每人每日都以各种形式接触着会计学。会计是各类现代企业的一个基本且重要的元素。它运用簿记的方法，对各种业务交易进行财务记录，并为企业提供关于资产、负债和经营成果等情况的财务报表。

作为一门"商业的语言"，会计学将企业的各种经济活动及决策结果与决策者联系在一起。无论是投资者、管理者还是业务决策者都需要了解相关会计条款和概念，因此会计人员的工作在国民经济的发展中起到了相当重要的作用。

古代会计学

在经济和文化的发展中占有重要地位的会计学有着如人类文明一样远古的历史。会计学极有可能产生于公元前大约4 000年的巴比伦，这里最早开始记录人类文明。巴比伦以商业城市而闻名，巴比伦人被视为一丝不苟的簿记员。他们喜欢将事情详细地记录在账目上。他们做这些精确记录的主要目的是揭示欺诈行为和提高办事效率。

与其他现代职业不同，会计创新者中很少有著名的人物。事实上，在意大利文艺复兴之前没有任何这方面的记录。最早系统介绍的簿记方法称为"复式记账法"，它出现在1494年，也就是哥伦布发现美洲的两年之后。它的提出者是Luca Pacioli，一位圣方济会的修道士，被认为是会计学之父。他所著的《算术、几何、比及比例概要》一书不但是最重要的数学论著之一，而且在会计领域上产生了前所未有的重大影响。

在这个领域中，最早知名的英文论著是1543年在伦敦出版的John Gouge的书。书中使用了一种方便的方式去描述簿记记录的次序，即：借方和贷方。此后，在1635年，一本名为《商人的镜子》的书出版了。在书中，作者引用了古代拉丁文簿记的例子，并解释道"账本的一边作为借方，另一边作为贷方"。这本书完整地论述了会计科学，它以详细精确的解释证明会计学早在17世纪就已被运用。

现代会计学

虽然会计始于远古的文明，但是它是在工业革命后才在社会上发挥重要作用的。在19世纪的工业革命时期，那些排挤掉了个体手工业的企业需要大量的资金资助。机器的运用能够生产大量同种产品，这就使企业需要计算大批量产品成本，而不是简单计算小规模个体手工产品的成本。为了满足分析各类成本和记录技术的需要,出现了成本会计这一新的会计领域。

随着制造业企业的扩大及复杂化,随着制造商之间的竞争加剧,企业管理需要更复杂的会计分析技术来衡量生产效率、制订未来生产计划等。20世纪计算机的出现更加速了这种进程。

当前,会计正处于迅速转变的时期。会计学正在从包括簿记及其相关预算和财务账目工作的传统领域不断扩展,其社会角色也显得越来越重要了。环境的变化不仅扩大了会计工作的内容,同时也影响了会计领域的界定。为此,在当下会计的起源和发展应该受到更多的关注,只有这样才能使我们更好地了解会计的社会影响以及如今会计人员从事工作的基础。

1.2 经济主体(我国称为会计主体)

经济主体是指会计为之服务的特定单位。经济主体按其法律地位的不同可分为以下几种类型。

独资经营企业

独资经营企业是由一个所有者经营的企业,是最简单的经济实体形式。单个所有者对企业的经营管理拥有唯一控制权。其管理费用十分低廉。然而,独资企业也是企业经济实体中最受限制的一种形式。所有的经营债务为其所有者个人义务。他必须亲自负担企业的合同、税务,以及由雇员在雇佣期间不正当行为而产生的法定负债。在融资方面独资企业也受到限制。当他进行负债融资时可能会遇到困难,除非他在某种程度上以个人财产做贷款抵押。

普通合伙企业

普通合伙企业通过书面的协议而建立,并在这样的共识基础上管理各合伙人的关系。合伙人通常共同享有企业的有形资产和无形资产。而且,每一个独立的合伙人应根据合伙合同约定的利益分配方式来分享企业的收益或损失。合伙人通过自有资本筹集企业的股权资金。当有新合伙人进入,或者是要在现有合伙关系中重新调整所有者权益时,合伙人应按照他们的出资额享有等比的权益。

普通合伙企业对经营债务承担无限个人责任。每一个合伙人都必须对经营的合同和民事侵权债务承担责任。另外,大多数的合伙协议都会限制合伙人退出合伙企业和转让合伙所有权的权利。

融资,尤其是长期融资,对于小型合伙企业来说常常是困难的。

有限责任合伙企业

有限责任合伙企业在某些方面与普通合伙企业相似,在另一些方面与股份公司相似。有限责任合伙企业这种经营方式通常只用于某些特定的行业,如律师或注册会计师,其中一个或多个合伙人对合伙制的债务和负债承担有限责任。这种债务保护的代价是对管理参与程度要有所限制。

股份公司

股份公司是根据特定的商业经营方面的法律条文成立的法人实体。在法律上,股份公司与其所有者是两个完全独立的实体。因此,股东一般不需要为企业承担责任。股份公司为把大量的资金从众多业主手中汇集到一起提供了更大的机会。然而,这种形式也有一些缺点,例如,维持公司机构运转需大量费用和管理负担，公司的经营利润要支付双倍的税额，当公司解散时资本收益也要支付双倍税额等。

1.3 会计假设

会计随着时间的推移而发展，随着社会的需求而变化。当贸易和商业活动中出现新的交易类型时，为记录这些交易，会计人员逐步建立了各种规则和惯例。构成会计的最基本概念是：

（1）经济主体假设（我国称为会计主体假设）

经济主体假设是指会计所核算的是一个特定的企业或单位的经济活动。企业是一个与其所有者分离的独立经济实体，因此公司的财务与所有者的财务不能混合核算。而且，经济主体和法律主体不是同一概念。

（2）持续经营假设

持续经营假设是指假设企业能持续存在很长的一段时间。大多数会计方法的使用是以两点为基础：一是企业是一个连续经营的经济主体，二是企业能够在可预见的未来继续维持运营。

持续经营假设适用于大多数的企业状况。只有当企业马上就要面临破产时，持续经营假设将不再适用。

（3）货币计量假设

会计核算应以货币为计量单位并假设币值不变。

（4）会计期间假设

会计期间假设是指一个企业的经济活动可以人为地划分为不同的期间。会计期间可以是一个财政年度、一个季度或一个月，其起讫日期可采用公历日期。

1.4 会计信息质量要求

（1）客观性原则

会计记录和财务报告应当以实际发生的财务和经济交易为依据。根据客观性原则，当期会计报表中列示的会计记录必须有实质意义并且可以确认，会计的个人偏见或人为选择不能影响会计核算的过程。

（2）可比性原则

会计记录和财务报告应当按照规定的会计处理方法进行，企业的会计信息应当相互可比、便于分析。

（3）相关性原则

企业提供的会计信息应当能够反映其财务状况、经营结果和现金流量，以满足会计信息使用者的需要。

（4）及时性原则

会计记录和财务报告的编制应当及时进行，不得提前或延后。

（5）明晰性原则

会计记录和财务报告应当清晰明了，便于理解、检查和使用。财务报告应当综合反映企业的财务状况和经营结果。

（6）谨慎性原则

谨慎性原则要求合理核算可能发生的损失和费用。根据这个原则，不明确收入不被计算，但是不确定的损失应充分估算。这条原则对企业可能存在的内部风险做了充分的考虑。

（7）重要性原则

企业应当在会计核算过程中，评估交易或事项的重要程度，以确定采用何种核算方式。重要会计事项必须按照规定的会计方法和程序进行处理，并在财务会计报告中充分、准确地予以披露。

（8）实质重于形式原则

企业应当按照交易或事项的经济实质进行会计核算，而不应当仅仅以它们的法律形式作为会计核算的依据。

第二单元　账户与复式记账

2.1　会计科目与账户

一个会计系统包含各种会计记录（支票簿、日记账、分类账等）以及一系列的过程和程序。它的目标是保证企业的各种财务数据和经济交易恰当地记入会计记录，以及保证企业的经营管理所需的财务报表是准确合宜的。一个会计系统通常包括以下几个部分：

会计科目表

为企业建立一个会计系统的第一个步骤是确定想要记录下的数据是什么。会计科目表简言之就是一张记录会计账户名称的列表，每项企业经营活动都按照指定的条目进行记录。会计科目表有两个组成部分。一个是科目代码，另一个是科目名称。对于大多数企业来讲，四位数字的科目代码已经足够；然而，一些业务更为复杂的企业有时也会使用六位数的科目代码。例如：

科 目 代 码	账 户 名 称	科 目 代 码	账 户 名 称
1001	现金	100201	银行存款——中国农业银行
1002	银行存款		

账户

一旦会计系统的账户建立好之后，与各种经营活动相关的交易信息都必须反映在账户上。账户是会计学中记录经营交易的最基本单位。它是用以记录企业财务报表上各项目的增减额的一种工具。管理层都要通过查阅账户来了解公司的财务状况和制订未来的发展计划。

简化的账户因为形似字母"T"而被称为T形账户。账户名称写在T形账户的上方。字母T的左边定义为"借方"，而右边定义为"贷方"。借方可以被缩写为"Dr."，贷方可以被缩写为"Cr."。T形账户的图示如下：

账户名称	
左方或称借方 (Dr.)	右方或称贷方 (Cr.)

账户的种类

1. 总分类账账户

总分类账,也称名义分类账,是会计活动的主要档案。它包含会计科目表的每一个账户,而且按照科目表上的科目顺序编排。总分类账中记录了企业的所有交易。它不是将企业当期的每一项活动都进行记录,而是反映交易的总数。它通常分为资产、负债、所有者权益、收入和费用五大类。

总分类账账户格式包括日期、摘要、每个账户的余额等,如下表所示:

账户名称　　　　　　　　　　　　　　　　　　　　　　　　账户代码_____

日　期	摘　要	借　方	贷　方	余　额

因为每一笔交易在一个账户记入借方,而在另一个账户以相同的数额记入贷方,所以总分类账账户总额总是平衡的,除非某个账户(有时称 T 形账户)出现误删或入错账的情况。资产负债表和利润表的数字来源于总分类账。由于总分类账是由独立的账户组成,所以它可以用来查看在任何给定时段影响每个账户的所有交易的数据。

2. 明细分类账账户

每一个明细分类账账户(SL)都支持一个独立的总分类账账户(GL),并通过采用账户代码表现出来。这种代码建立起总分类账账户与明细分类账账户之间的联系。它们的联系方式主要有两种:

一个总分类账账户对应一个明细分类账账户:这种联系中,总分类账账户的余额由单个明细分类账账户而更新。明细分类账账户为总分类账账户提供详细的资料,以帮助经营者了解影响本账户财务状况的所有交易情况。在这种情况下,总分类账账户与明细分类账账户往往有相同的账户名称。

一个总分类账账户对应多个明细分类账账户:在这样的联系中,总分类账账户的数额由几个明细分类账账户共同更新。这种结构有利于对现金余额的高一级监管。例如,为了监管"银行存款"账户,我们可以建立几个相关的明细分类账户,如"银行存款——中国农业银行""银行存款——中国银行"和"银行存款——中国建设银行"。

2.2　会计要素与会计恒等式

为了更好地学习财务会计,需要了解会计要素和会计恒等式。什么是会计要素?会计要素

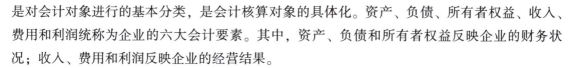

是对会计对象进行的基本分类，是会计核算对象的具体化。资产、负债、所有者权益、收入、费用和利润统称为企业的六大会计要素。其中，资产、负债和所有者权益反映企业的财务状况；收入、费用和利润反映企业的经营结果。

资产

资产是企业拥有或控制的能以货币计量的经济资源，包括所有财产、债权和其他权利。资产通常分为流动资产、长期投资、固定资产、无形资产、递延资产和其他资产。流动资产是指可以在一年或者超过一年的一个营业周期内变现或者耗用的资产。长期投资是指不能或不准备在一年内变现的投资。固定资产是指使用年限在一年以上，单位价值在规定标准以上，并在使用过程中保持原来物质形态的资产。无形资产是指企业长期使用而没有实物形态的资产。递延资产是指不能全部计入当年损益，而应当在以后年度内分期摊销的各项费用。其他资产是指除以上各项目以外的资产。

负债

负债是企业所承担的能以货币计量、需以资产或劳务偿付的债务。它与你拥有的有价资产形成明显的对比。可以说"资产是往你口袋中放入现金，而负债则是将现金从你口袋中取走"。负债分为流动负债和长期负债。流动负债是指将在一年或者超过一年的一个营业周期内偿还的债务，包括短期借款、应付票据、应付账款、预收货款、应付工资、应交税金、应付股利、其他应付款等。长期负债是指偿还期在一年或者超过一年的一个营业周期以上的债务，包括长期借款、应付债券、长期应付款项等。

所有者权益

所有者权益是投资人对企业净资产的所有权，包括投资人对企业投入的资本以及形成的资本公积金、盈余公积金和未分配利润等。在股份公司中，所有者权益也被称为股东权益。

收入

收入是企业在销售商品或者提供劳务等经营业务中实现的资金流入，包括基本营业收入和其他营业收入。

费用

费用是企业在生产经营过程中发生的各项耗费，表现为本期资产的流出或消耗或是负债的产生。费用的增加会减少所有者权益。收入和费用是所有者权益项目下的两大分支。

利润

利润是企业在一定会计期间的经营成果，包括营业利润、投资净收益和营业外收支净额。当收入超过费用时，将产生净收益；反之，将产生净损失。

会计恒等式

上述会计要素相互之间的关系可用一个简单的数学公式表示，这个公式就是会计恒等式：

$$资产 = 负债 + 所有者权益$$

在算式中，所有者权益等于总资产减去总负债。因此，所有者权益也称为净资产。

企业最初的时候，所有者权益只受实收资本如发行股本的影响。企业开始经营之后，就会出现收益（收入减去费用，所得减去损失），也可能出现新增的资本，或因分配股利等而减少资本。所以，当会计期间结束时，这些因素对所有者权益的影响如下：

$$资产 = 负债 + 期初所有者权益 + （收入 - 费用）$$

最后，这个恒等式在代数变换后如下：

$$资产 + 费用 = 负债 + 期初所有者权益 + 收入$$

这一公式无论在什么时候都恒成立。如果等式成立，则可以说会计账户是平衡的。如果账户出现不平衡，则说明发生了会计失误。

2.3 复式记账

复式记账法的定义

复式记账法是记录交易的一种方法，这种方法记账准确，便于核对。例如：

（1）ABC 公司为支付电话费而做的分录如下：

管理费用　　　　　$50　　　（借方表示费用增加）

现金　　　　　　　$50　　　（贷方表示资产减少）

（2）电话公司对同一笔交易（在从电话公司的角度）做的分录如下：

现金　　　　　　　$50　　　（借方表示资产增加）

主营业务收入　　　$50　　　（贷方表示收入增加）

复式记账法的规则

规则一：二元性规则

每一项交易都有两方。借方记录在一个账户，贷方记录在另一个账户，借贷必须相等。因为借贷双方相等，所以复式记账法能够避免某些普通记账失误。

规则二：方向性规则

大多数人认为贷方就是减数，借方就是加数，但是很多账户并非如此。为了进行区别，我们称之为借方账户和贷方账户。

所有的资产类和费用类账户都是借方账户，也就是说它们是正数。换句话说，在复式记账系统中资产是正的。负债账户是贷方账户，它们是负的，但通常在资产负债表上它们并不标以减号。所有者权益和收入类账户也都是贷方账户。费用类账户都是借方账户。

以下的表格归纳了借贷方对不同账户的影响。

账户类型	借方	贷方	账户类型	借方	贷方
资产	增加	减少	收入	减少	增加
负债	减少	增加	费用	增加	减少
所有者权益	减少	增加			

总结为：

（1）借记表示资产增加，负债和所有者权益减少；

（2）贷记表示负债和所有者权益增加，资产减少。

规则三：借方在左边，贷方在右边

每一笔交易至少都有一个贷方和一个借方。通常，企业账户的其中一个是资产负债账户。没有记入资产负债账户的账目就一定要记进收益或支出账户。

2.4 会计循环

会计程序是指起始于商业交易并结束于结账的一系列活动。由于每一会计期间都必须重复这一程序，所以它又被称为会计循环。

第一步：根据基础业务文件即原始凭证分析各项交易，并记入记账凭证。

对企业进行的每一笔交易都要编制某种原始凭证，例如销售发票、收据、提货单、订购单等。在记账凭证内登记交易称为做分录。所记录的每一笔交易都是一项分录；它遵循复式记账原则，并且必须由特定人员对其进行严格的检查和核准。

第二步：将数据从记账凭证转入明细分类账账户。

每一项经济交易都必须根据会计凭证科学、完整、连续地记录进会计账簿，这个过程称为过账。借方、贷方连同凭证日期、凭证中记录交易的摘要和每张凭证的编号一起转入。某些特定类型的频繁交易需要记入序时的账本，称为日记账。一些特别账户包括现金账户和银行存款账户，不仅需要记入明细分类账，还需要记入每天的日记账。

第三步：根据明细分类账的账户余额编制试算平衡表。

记入各分类账的借方金额和贷方金额是否相等，可用试算平衡表验证。试算平衡表列示的所有账户将按其出现在明细分类账中的顺序排序。如果账户余额计算正确，结果产生各账户的借方余额总额一定等于各账户贷方余额总额。为了验证分类账中的借方金额与贷方金额是否相等，可以在任何时候编制试算平衡表。

第四步：将数据从明细分类账账户转入总分类账账户。

总分类账是由按财务报表要素进行分类的独立账户构成。当从明细分类账过账到总分类账时，往往将应记入某一账户的所有记录都相加起来，作为一笔总计数过账。

第五步：编制调整分录，将某些账户的余额调整为合乎配比原则的恰当金额。

在每一个会计分期期末，往往必须对某些账户余额进行调整，以使成本及费用能与收入进行恰当的配比。这些分录将收入摊配到各个赚取期，将费用摊配到使用相关产品和服务的各个消耗期。

第六步：编制财务报表。

一旦做出恰当的调整分录并过入分类账户之后，便可直接根据各账户的余额编制利润表和资产负债表。然而在实务中，许多会计人员发现，先草拟一张工作底表可以方便财务报表的编制。

工作底表是一种多栏式表格，会计人员可用以汇总调整分录及编制财务报表所需的信息，但它不可以替代财务报表或任何会计分录。如果工作底表没有被采用，那么财务报表的数据将直接来源于调整后的分类账账户。

第七步：结账。

结账是在会计期末进行的最后一个步骤。临时账户或名义账户应留存下来以编制利润表。一旦本年的会计报表编制完毕,通过把临时性账户的余额结转入另一名为本年利润的账户,即可将其结清。

第三单元　流动资产

3.1　现金

公司拥有的或具所有权的一切资源统称为资产。公司的资产有流动资产、固定资产及其他形式资产。流动资产通常是指公司资产中的现金,或者未来一年或超过一年的一个经营周期之内可转为现金的部分,如现金、应收款、存货、有价证券、预付费用以及短期投资。由于在公司面临破产时流动资产易于清算,所以公司债权人常常关注公司流动资产的多少。而且对大多数公司来说,流动资产作为其日常运营的资金来源非常重要。主要的流动资产有现金、应收款和存货。

什么是现金?

常规意义上的现金指的是钱柜里的纸币、硬币以及银行存款。会计中所指的现金包括库存的货币(含铸币、纸币)和存放在银行或其他存储机构的货币。此外,那些随时到期的正式流通票据都可以被归类为会计意义上的现金,包括银行汇票、银行本票、商业汇票、保付支票和普通意义上的支票。在会计报表中,现金是最活跃的项目,通常被称为速动资产。可用以下特点来解释现金:

- 它容易转换成其他资产,是公司拥有的流动性最强的资产。
- 现金容易隐藏和转移。它是一项最容易被挪用、被滥用的资产。

有些企业在报告现金时采用"现金和现金等价物"这一术语。留作特殊用途的现金应依据它的使用时间,分别报告为流动资产或是固定资产。如果留作特殊用途的现金预期在未来一年内使用,那么它应报告为流动资产。否则,则应报告为长期投资。邮票和未到期支票(未来应付支票)等项目不是现金。邮票报告为预付费用,而未到期支票是应收账款。

现金控制系统

现金控制系统的基本内容有:

(1) 规定现金使用范围

收录的许多业务交易应采用现金,例如:

- 支付职工个人的工资、津贴、奖金和额外福利费用等。
- 出差人员的差旅费。
- 其他零星支出,包括邮费、送货服务费以及器具用具的小额购买。

(2) 控制库存现金额度

不少公司发现为小额开支签发支票既不方便也很浪费,所以保持一定量的库存现金能方便日常零星开支。这笔零用现金储备的多寡视公司的具体情形而定。大多数企业留存的现金能够维持三至四周的零用开支。

因为现金交易量大且交易频繁，在操作现金和做账过程中可能会出现很多差错。为了保证会计记录的准确性和可靠性，有必要进行有效的现金内部控制。现金控制系统是企业内部控制系统的一部分，具有两大主要职能。

1. **现金收入的内部控制**

大部分企业现金流入的来源有许多。用来实现有效控制的手段也各有不同。然而，在任何情况下下述几种途径都很重要：

- 及时核算每一笔现金收入。
- 及时记录每一笔现金收入。
- 按时存储所有的现金收入。

2. **现金支出的内部控制**

大部分企业的现金支出原因也有许多，如用于支付费用、购买资产等。在支出过程中滥用现金的事件因相对容易掩盖而时有发生，除非有一个有效控制系统，例如：

- 除了采用备用金制度来应对小额支付外，用支票支付所有的现金支出。支票的签署、保管、开票（有时候还有邮寄）工作彼此独立进行。专人专事才能达到最有效控制。要实现有效的现金内部控制，第一步是确立责任、划分义务。
- 建立备用金制度并进行严格控制与监督。
- 支票提前编号，只有出示认可发票时才签发支票。
- 严格管理所有的现金支付、账簿保管和内部定期报告，定期或不定期地由独立第三方对其进行核实。

银行往来调节表

一般来说，为方便交易，也为了对现金实现更有效的控制，企业会在银行开设存款账户。大部分情况下，现金通过银行流入和流出，日常现金收入存入银行，这样尽可能减少了手头现金量。而且，银行每月向企业出示对账单，说明期初存款余额、本月内每一笔存款业务和取款业务，以及月末存款余额。公司将银行对账单与公司内部现金记录进行比较，然后确定两者之间是否有差异和错误，并找出原因。各项差异和错误都在银行往来调节表中予以记录和校正。

3.2 应收款

由于很大一部分交易和买卖是按赊销方式进行的，所以公司应密切注意并且妥善管理应收款。存在多个赊购客户的企业需设立应收款总分类账，同时为每个赊购客户设立一个独立账户。"应收款"这一术语指的是一年或超过一年的一个经营期内可向个人或其他企业（实体）收回的款项。应收款包括应收账款、应收票据和应收非营业账款。下面将按照资产负债表上列出的顺序逐一予以讨论和阐述：

应收账款

应收账款是用于记录由于销售商品或提供服务而产生的应向客户收取的款项的账户。应收账款通常有望在正常营业期内无条件转变为现金。本单元将着重讨论折扣和坏账，这两项构成了对应收账款进行会计处理的主要组成部分。

折扣

生产商或中间商常给采购商尤其是给批发商提供折扣。折扣有两种：商业折扣和现金折扣。

商业折扣是卖方主要以促销为目的提供的减价。买方直接以发票价（标价减去一定量的折扣）为其所购商品或劳务付款。所以商业折扣无需记录，也无法在账目中显示出来。

现金折扣对卖方来说是一种销售折扣，是用来作为一种招揽订单的竞争手段，或作为一种鼓励即时付款的激励方式。在销售协议中，它通常紧跟在价格后面以两种方式表述：每件价格为\$×××，10日内支付给1%折扣，10日以后1个月以内则按原价支付；或者每件价格为\$×××，10日内支付给3%的折扣，10日以后50日以内则按原价支付。现金折扣有两种可选的记录方式：总价法和净价法。

按总价法，会计将应收账款与销售额以发票价入账。如果买方最终享受了折扣，作为单独一项的"销售折扣"将用来记录实收现金与应收账款之间的差额。反之，不会记录现金折扣。在卖方能确定当交易发生时买方即会享受现金折扣的情况下，通常采用净价法。这样，净销售额（发票价减去现金折扣）即会同时记入应收账款与销售额账目。

坏账

在对商品和劳务进行赊销时，由于各种原因，必然会出现一部分到期无法收回的应收账款。因不能收回应收账款而产生的营业费用或营业损失称为坏（呆）账损失。这类费用或损失是赊销业务中正常的且不可避免的一大风险。通常情况下，对不可收回的应收账款有下述两种记账方法。

1. 直接冲销法

用直接冲销法时，当一项应收账款确认不可收回且费用或损失得以证实时，坏账才被入账。卖方通过将其作为一笔当期费用来冲销这笔账款。显然，按照这种方法，收益在当期入账，而坏账损失却在另一个会计期间做出。使用这种会计方法的结果是，利润表和资产负债表均无法准确反映公司财务状况，这些报表也不能作为永远有效的财务分析指标。

2. 备抵法

因为直接冲销法存在缺陷，很多数额重大的坏账费用都以备抵法做账。备抵法需要按期对不可回收账款进行估计。用备抵法时，对不可回收账款的估计值在会计期末以调整分录做出。这样，坏账能更好、更准确地对应于利润表和资产负债表。

应收票据

应收票据是一方向另一方签发的在规定时间内无条件还款的书面承诺。相对应收账款而言，卖方更倾向于应收票据，因为它有下述优点：

- 应收票据是对出票人或其受让人的强制性法律要求权。
- 在到期之前的任何时候都可以向银行申请将票据贴现。也是由于这个原因，应收票据账款在资产负债表中列于应收账款项前。
- 带息票据有利息可收。

应收非营业账款

应收账款和应收票据是由买卖商品和提供服务产生的，它们通常被认为是企业拥有的最为重要的应收款。这两项合起来称为应收营业账款。应收非营业账款，顾名思义，指的是销售非商品资产而产生的应收款以及与任何销售或交易无关的其他形式的短期应收款。例如给官员或公司员工提供的贷款、应收的利息和股利以及向保险公司索赔等。

3.3 存货

存货的定义和类型

存货是流动资产的一种，用来指代在未来一年内或一个较长的经营周期中变现或在生产中被消耗的商品或材料。在经济生活中，存货是商业活动的重要晴雨表。企业应该密切关注并指明存货数量及出售或耗用库存货物所需的时间。同时，存货应保持适量，不宜过多也不宜过少。公司存货过少无法满足需求会使其错失销售良机，也会令生产下降。而存货过量的公司则会背负不必要的置存成本。在会计中，存货会影响资产负债表，因为它通常是最重要的一项流动资产。存货也会以决定一定时期内生产量的方式影响到利润表。

商品库存是指那些归公司所有的、日常经营活动中为了销售而购入的商品。而对于制造商来说，存货不一定都是用来出售的。制造商的存货由以下几项构成：

- 用于生产的原材料。
- 在制造过程中的半成品。
- 待运输给客户的产成品。
- 价格低廉的易耗用品。

存货盘存制度

在会计实务中，有两种库存管理系统可供企业选择：永续盘存制和定期盘存制。根据永续盘存制，每一笔存货入库与发出的数量和金额都应详细记录。这一系统连续动态地提供了各种货物现有库存的存货记录。尽管如此，永续盘存记录的准确性仍然必须通过一年至少一次的对各种商品的盘点来加以验证。然后将这些记录同库存商品实际数量相对照，并对出现的差异进行调整。

一些企业认为投资建立一个计算机化的永续盘存系统既没有必要也太浪费。许多小型商业经营者也觉得用永续盘存制不划算。而按照定期盘存制，只需登记每次销售的销货收入。销售时对已售商品的成本不做记录。因此，已销售产品的成本只会在每个会计期末通过实物盘存按期结账。

存货计价

确定销售产品的成本包含两个重要方面：确定各项库存的数量与确定每项库存的单位成本。关于存货单位成本的计算，有如下三种常用方法。

（1）后进先出法

后进先出法假设首先销售最近购入的商品，因此，最近购货的单位成本即被认为是待销售货物的单位成本。这种方法常用于对大宗商品如沙、煤炭等的成本计价。

(2) 平均法（又称加权平均法）

按照平均法，已销售商品与存货的单位成本是一致的。平均价格由以下公式得出：平均单位价格＝商品总成本/总数量。

(3) 个别辨认法

个别辨认法最适用于高价格的存货项目，如汽车、建筑设备等。如果存货产品的单位价值低而且数量又多，个别辨认法就难以实行。

第四单元　非流动资产

4.1　长期投资

长期投资是指不准备在一年内变现的投资，包括股票投资、债券投资和其他投资。企业购买同行或其他愿意涉足的行业的股份，是为实现一定的战略目标，如控制竞争对手或拓展新业务等。股票投资和其他投资应当根据不同情况，分别采用成本法或权益法进行核算。本单元要讨论的是如何计量和报告对普通股以及对债券的长期投资。

普通股投资的计量和报告

普通股投资的会计处理是基于投资公司对被投资公司的经营和财务方面的影响力度而言的。

持有被投资公司不到20%的普通股的投资公司不能对被投资公司施加重大影响，这时采用成本法。当采用此方法时，投资按成本入账，而且只有在得到分红时才计入收益。

但是，如果投资方拥有另一公司的20%以上50%以下的普通股，则需采用权益法，采用此方法时股票的购买与成本法一样按成本入账，但投资者以不同于成本法的方式记录其按份额享有的被投资公司的每期净收益和现金或实物股利。持20%到50%股份的投资方可对被投资方的财务和经营活动施加重大影响。投资方有权派一名代表出席被投资方的董事会。投资方通过这种方式对被投资方实施一定的控制权。

对另一实体持有50%及以上的普通股的公司被称为母公司。母公司因其股份所有权而对子公司（或附属公司）拥有控股权。这种情况下通常会准备一套合并财务报表。合并财务报表上会显示母公司控制的所有资产和负债以及子公司的所有收益和费用。

债券投资的计量和报告

债券投资应当按实际支付的款项记账。溢价或者折价购入的债券，其实际支付的价款与债券面值的差额，应当在债券到期前分期摊销。债券投资存续期内的应计利息，以及出售时收回的本息与债券账面成本及尚未收回应计利息的差额，应当计入当期损益。股票、债券和其他各种投资应按其账面余额在会计报表中分别予以记录。

4.2　固定资产（不动产、厂房和设备）

固定资产包括土地（根据我国相关法律，在会计中土地被视为一项无形资产）、房屋及建筑物、机器设备、运输设备、工具和器具等。

固定资产的特点综述如下：
- 使用年限较长，相对耐用（通常使用年限超过一年）。
- 单位价值在规定标准以上。
- 使用过程中原来的物质形态保持不变。

固定资产的购置成本

在购置日，固定资产应遵循成本原则来计量并按成本入账。成本包含资产购置和使其发挥既有用途所必需的所有费用。土地成本包含现金购入价外加相关转让费用，如产权费、律师费、房地产经纪人佣金以及应计的财产税。建筑物的成本包含合同价外加建筑设计师报酬、建筑许可费以及开发成本。至于大型设备和器具，购入价及其他相关费用，如营业税、运费、由买方支付的运输保险费等，应包含在其成本中。除此之外，相对大额的设备装配、安装、调试、维护和修理、翻新和改良等费用也应该视为固定资产成本的组成部分，而小额支出则作为当期运营费用处理。

固定资产折旧

固定资产购置之后，必须在账目中计量资产在有效年限内的使用费用。固定资产除土地外均应计提折旧。折旧是资产在使用年限内因磨损或因技术老化，逐渐转移到产品或服务的成本中去的那一部分价值。折旧也可指成本分摊的过程。在计算固定资产折旧时应考虑四个因素：
- 成本，即购置资产和使其准备发挥既有用途所必需的所有费用。
- 使用年限，资产的预期使用寿命，也称"服务年限"。
- 残值，对资产在使用年限结束时剩余价值的估计。
- 总产量，对资产工作量的估计（如机器的运作时间，卡车的行驶里程等）。

折旧方法

1. **直线折旧法**

在直线折旧法下，一项固定资产在其使用年限内每年的年折旧额都相等。从这个角度讲，直线折旧法又被称为"平均年限法"。当固定资产在每一个会计期间均匀使用时经常采用直线折旧法，这样也比较合理。假定ABC公司以$15 000的价格购置了一项固定资产，预期使用年限为四年，预期残值为$800。

ABC公司固定资产折旧进度表

年份	折旧成本	折旧率	年折旧额	累计折旧	账面价值
1	$14 200	25%	$3 550	$3 550	$11 450
2	$14 200	25%	$3 550	$7 100	$7 900
3	$14 200	25%	$3 550	$10 650	$4 350
4	$14 200	25%	$3 550	$14 200	$800（残值）

注：折旧成本＝成本－残值

折旧率＝100%/使用年限

年折旧额＝折旧成本×折旧率

账面价值＝成本－累计折旧

2. 产量折旧法

产量折旧法把折旧与资产使用以及资产带来的产出联系起来,而与使用时间没有关联。产量折旧法下折旧额是由当年的实际产量乘以单位折旧成本得出的。这种折旧法特别用于资产的使用程度在各期很不均匀的一些行业。上例中,如果 ABC 公司所购资产预期带来的总产量是 100 000 件(第一、二、三、四年分别为 5 000 件、55 000 件、35 000 件和 5 000 件),那么这种方式下的折旧进度应如下表所示。

ABC 公司固定资产折旧进度表

年份	单位折旧成本	年产量	年折旧额	累计折旧	账面价值
1	$0.142	5 000	$710	$710	$14 290
2	$0.142	55 000	$7 810	$8 520	$6 480
3	$0.142	35 000	$4 970	$13 490	$1 510
4	$0.142	5 000	$710	$14 200	$800(残值)

注:年折旧额 = 单位折旧成本 × 年产量

还有一种折旧方法是加速折旧法,这一方法又包括双倍余额递减法、年数总和法、固定比率折旧法和成本递减法。无论采用哪种方法,目的都在于能最恰当地计量固定资产在使用年限内对收入的贡献。方法一旦选定,就应该始终如一地运用于整个资产使用年限中。

使用期间的开销

如前所述,在固定资产的使用年限内可能出现各种各样的支出。

1. 营业支出

为保证资产的运转效率及其生产寿命和生产量而进行的常规维修会给公司带来各种支出。例如,给车加油,更换办公楼管道设备和更换机器设备旧齿轮等。这些频繁出现的较小金额的成本记在营业支出下。

2. 资本支出

相反,那些以提高资产运转效率、增加生产寿命和生产量为目的的不常发生的大金额的增添和改进成本被视为资本支出。

固定资产的处置

固定资产可能以报废、出售或更新的方式予以处置。在处置固定资产时,必须确定其账面价值。不管以何种方式处置固定资产,都应将其账面价值和处置收入进行比较,得出"处置利得"或"处置损失"。二者都将被记录到当期的利润表中。

4.3 无形资产

无形资产的定义和特征

无形资产是指那些没有实物形态的长期资产,这类资产因其所有者独占某种权利和特权而有价值,主要包括专利权、版权、商标和商号权、特许权等。无形资产具有以下几个重要特点。

(1)不具有实物形态

不具有实物形态是无形资产的首要特征和主要确认依据。这一特征使无形资产有别于固定资产。

（2）可以长期使用

一项无形资产可以在不止一个会计期间内为主体带来收益。这一特征使之有别于流动资产，从而被界定为非流动资产。

（3）具有垄断性

无形资产通常是属于单个主体的独占权利。无形资产的独占权受法律或其他政府法规的保护而不与他人共享。

（4）收益具有不确定性

无形资产所带来的收益额很难预计。而且，无形资产收益与其他资产带来的收益也很难区分。因而很难单独地确定相应的收益额。

购入的无形资产应当按实际成本记账。接受投资取得的无形资产，应当按照评估值或者合同约定的金额记账。自行开发的无形资产，应当按开发过程中实际发生的成本记账。各种无形资产应当在受益期内分期平均摊销，未摊销余额在会计报表中列示。

专利权

专利权由有关政府机构（国家知识产权局）授予，赋予专利所有人独享专利权20年。

版权

版权由政府机构授予，版权所有者独享发行、再版以及销售其文字作品和其他形式的艺术作品的权利，有效期为作者寿命加50年。

商标和商号权

商标和商号是用来标识某个企业或某种产品的字、词或符号，例如，"联想""可口可乐"以及用来代表"麦当劳"的大写字母"M"等。商标和商号对企业及其产品的声望、销量起重要作用。

特许权

特许权是由政府或公司授予个人或组织的在指定地域内开展特定商业活动的特权。如允许使用城市街道特许运营一条公交线路，以及在某个地区销售某些产品的经销权等，都属于特许权。

第五单元 负　　债

5.1 流动负债

流动负债的定义及分类

负债是企业所承担的能以货币计量、需以资产或劳务向债权人偿付的债务。负债一般分为流动负债和长期负债。

流动负债是指将在需要时用现有流动资产或通过产生其他流动负债来偿还的一种债务。与流动资产一样，流动负债的偿还时间不超过一年或更长的一个会计期间。流动负债包括：

（1）应付票据与应付账款

一年内到期的应付票据和应付账款计入流动负债。只要取得银行贷款，企业就要签发应付票据。在其他一些情况下，企业也可签发应付票据，这些情况包括购买不动产或昂贵的设备，有时也包括购买其他物品。票据可以是短期的也可以是长期的，这由它的付款期所决定。票据还分为附息票据和无息票据。

应付账款指由于购买商品或获得服务而对供应商承担的短期负债。这种信贷的期限通常写在销售条款中（如2/10，n/30），并且一般以30天到60天为限。

（2）应计费用

应计费用包括应付租金、应付税费、应付利息，以及员工和工人的工资、奖金及福利费用。

（3）未获收益

未获收益是指未交货商品、未提供服务时已获得的收益。

（4）本年内到期的长期负债

将于一年内到期偿还的长期负债，应当在流动负债下单列项目反映。

（5）或有负债

债务及债务量仍不能确定，且据未来情形可能发生。由于未来事件的发生，或有负债有可能变成一项现实的债务，也有可能完全消除。例如所得税和由售后产品的保修而引起的负债等。

流动负债可按其金额是否确定而进行分类，具体分为可确定金额的流动负债、估计负债以及或有负债。在资产负债表上，流动负债一般按照日期从早到晚的顺序或者金额从大到小的顺序排列。

流动比率

财务报表的使用者都会密切关注流动资产与流动负债之间的关系。这层关系在对一个公司的资产变现能力（清偿短期债务的能力）进行评估时很重要。当流动资产额超过流动负债额时，清偿债务的可能性就比较大。若情况相反，短期债务就可能无法偿还，或许最终迫使公司破产。流动资产除以流动负债得出流动比率。流动比率可用来比较不同企业之间的资产变现能力，也可比较同一企业不同时期的资产变现能力。流动比率越高，表示公司内部运作环境越健全，公司外部信用地位越好。例如，投资者会仔细地考虑和比较他（她）想投资的几家公司的流动比率，然后再做最终决定。同样地，供货商在打算赊销产品之前，银行还没有提供贷款的时候都不可能忽视客户的流动比率。连员工都会因为担心拖欠工资，而借此权衡选择在所在公司工作是否正确。流动比率是财务报表的外部使用者用以支持其决定或判断的必要信息来源。

5.2 长期负债

长期负债是指偿还期超过一年或者一个营业周期的债务，包括长期借款、应付债券、长期应付款项等。此外，递延所得税、员工养老保险、员工解雇费、休假补贴等也都属于长期负债。

长期借款

长期借款包括向金融机构和其他单位的借款。它应当按借款性质及实际发生的数额单独记账。

长期应付款

长期应付款包括进口设备应付款、融资租赁固定资产应付款等。长期应付款应当按实际发生数额记账。

经营租赁和融资租赁是租赁中较常见的两种。经营租赁中,财产所有权仍然归出租方所有,承租方只是暂时使用该项财产。所以在利润表中以费用的形式记录租金。但是在某些情况下,租赁合同将所有权的全部利益和风险转移给承租方。这时的租赁实际上就是购买资产。这种形式的租赁被称为融资租赁。融资租赁虽然在法律意义上是一种租赁行为,但在实际意义上是承租方的分期付款购买方式。在以下任一情形下,租赁被确认为融资租赁:

- 在租赁期间,承租方可选择以低于市场价格买进租赁资产,之后该资产所有权转给承租方。
- 租赁期达到或超过该资产使用寿命的75%。
- 租赁期内的租金总额达到或超过该资产市场价格的90%。

在上述情况中,租赁资产计入资产负债表的固定资产项下。次年应付的负债作为流动负债,而剩余部分归为长期负债。融资租赁是近年来国内外企业青睐的普通筹资方式。与用长期贷款购入固定资产相比,融资租赁手续简便,且投资成本可提前收回,因而更为可取。

应付债券

以上两种融资方式都涉及寻找一个愿意提供所需资金的个人、企业或金融机构。而发行债券是为了获得大额长期资本。债券有很多种,且各有其自身特点。有些债券的持有者可以选择将其转换成普通股,称为可转换债券。另外那些发行者可选择在到期前以一定金额赎回的债券,被称为可提前(可通知)赎回债券。此外,有明确作为担保的抵押资产的债券是担保债券,无担保债券是不具有明确作为担保的抵押资产的债券;定期债券在固定的到期日到期,分期还本债券在不同到期日分期偿还;还有根据是否以持有者名字签发来分的记名债券和不记名债券。无论哪种债券都是一种附息应付票据。

如果息票利率(即名义利率)与市场利率(实际利率)恰巧一致时,债券以票面价值销售。但是这种情况很少发生,因为市场利率经常变化,公司在印制债券时很难预测出售债券时的市场利率。所以债券经常不以票面价销售。如果息票利率低于市场利率则折价销售,如果市场利率低于息票利率则溢价销售。债券折价和溢价的摊销应在每个会计期间以直线摊销法或实际利率法单独记录和报告。因而债券折价销售并不代表发行者财务状况令人担忧,债券溢价销售也不能说就意味着其财务实力雄厚。长期债权人总是对公司偿息能力和到期偿付票面价值的能力特别关心。下面两个比值对投资方来说具有一定的参考价值:

(1)资产负债比

总负债额(包括流动负债和长期负债)除以总资产额得出资产负债比。资产负债比越高,公司无法按期偿债的可能性就越大。

（2）已获利息倍数

已获利息倍数代表公司支付到期利息的能力或用所得支付利息的程度，其计算公式是：息税前利润/利息费用。已获利息倍数越低，意味着能用来支付利息的收益越少，那么公司提高利息率的可能性就越小。

第六单元　所有者权益

6.1　股本

股份公司

通常来说，股份公司是一种如自然人一样拥有合法权利的独立、明确的实体。也就是说，股份公司能在其名下开设银行账户、拥有财产和从事经营活动。股份公司至少应有一名所有者，所有者的数量没有上限。

股份公司所有者也称为股东或股票持有者。股东的所有权利益以股份为单位计量。股份公司主要的优势在于其所有者个体不需要为该公司的债务承担责任。例如，如果一个股份公司被起诉且被迫宣布破产，其所有者并不会被要求用他们自己的钱去偿还公司债务。如果股份公司的资产不够偿还债务，债权人不得向该公司的股东、董事或高管人员追偿。

股份公司由董事会管理，董事会负责为本公司的重大事件做决定并管理日常事务。就像选国会议员那样，董事是由公司的股东选出的。而管理公司日常事务的高管人员则由董事会任命。

一个人能否成为股份公司股东取决于他是否购买了股票，而不取决于他与其他股东的人身关系。因此，股份公司能够迅速、广泛、大量地集中资金。虽然无限责任公司或有限责任公司的资本也都划分为股份，但是这些公司并不公开发行股票，其股份也不能自由转让。证券市场上发行和流通的股票都是由股份公司发行的。

股本亦称股份资本。股份公司的经济基础是股东认购的金额和财产。股份是构成股本的成分，并且是股本的计量单位。换句话说，股份公司的资金和财产的总额，即股本，是由股份构成的，且等于全部股份金额的总和。

股本包括普通股和优先股。

普通股

普通股在股份公司中代表所有权。一股就是一份所有权。如果一个公司发行10股，那么每一股就代表公司的10%的所有权；如果该公司发行100股，每一股则代表公司1%的所有权。这种股票使所有者除有权获得公司的一份利润外，还有权对公司的决策进行表决。当然，大多数的公司发行数以百万计的股票，使得每一股所含的权益只是公司股本总额极其微小的一份。这些股票是可以转让的，你每次进行的交易也就是股票的转让。

普通股的股利分为现金股利、股票股利和资产股利。最常见的分配方式是现金股利。公司董事会决定是否给普通股股东分配股利。股利的增加或减少取决于公司的经营状况。经营状况不良的公司甚至会推迟分配股利，直到它的资产负债表所显示的财政状况好转。

如果发行股票的公司破产且不得不卖掉它的资产，那么只有在其他所有的债权人、债券持有者和优先股的股东获得清算资产后，才轮到普通股的股东。

普通股股东享有的主要权利
- 在年度会议上对董事会的选举进行投票。
- 通过获取股息分享公司的收益。
- 发行新股时，保留同等份额的所有权。
- 根据所持股份的比例分享资产清算的利益。

优先股

优先股在股份公司里也代表所有权。优先股的持有者相对于普通股的持有者来说，享有某些优先权利。优先股经常享有如下权利：
- 股利分配的优先权。
- 破产时享有优先清偿权。
- 可以转换为普通股。

享有上述优先权利的交换条件是优先股股东不能在股东大会上表决或享有其他特定的权利。

股利的优先分配权并不保证公司一定会支付股利。它仅仅是保证公司在支付普通股股利之前，必须以一定股息率或适当金额先支付优先股的股利。

优先股可以是有面值股，也可以是无面值股。

有面值股是指在公司章程中分配了每股价值的股份资本。票面价值可以由公司决定为任何数额。通常，有面值股的票面价值数额很小，但与它的市场价无关。例如，某公司有面值股的票面价值为每股 1.25 美元，但它股票最近的市场价可能已经上涨到每股 80 美元。

其股利为面值的固定比率。例如，如果股票的面值为 100 元，年利息为 6%，那么年股利为每股 6 元。近年来，一些公司也开始发行股息率随银行利率变化的优先股。

6.2　留存收益

一个公司产生了利润后，管理层面临两种选择：或者把这些利润作为现金股利分配给股东，或者将收益留存并再投资于企业。

通常的处置方式是把利润的一部分以股利的形式分配给股东。剩下的称为留存收益或留存资金。

当管理者决定把收益进行留存时，他们必须在资产负债表的股东权益一栏进行结算，使投资者了解这些年来企业中投入了多少资金。如果一个公司把所有的收益都投入公司发展，但是并没有什么意外的高增长，那么可以肯定当公司董事会宣布分配股利时，这个公司的股东会有丰厚的回报。

任何成功的管理的最终目标都是每创造 1 元的市值就能有 1 元的留存收益。

投资者必须通过了解公司从股东那里保留了多少资金，来判断一个公司的基本面。为股东谋取利润应该是上市公司的主要目的,这样,投资者会更加注意公司的收益报告。利润固然重要,但是公司对利润的处理也同样重要。投资者应该密切注意公司如何使用留存资金及其产生的回报。

第七单元　收入、费用和利润

7.1　收入

对于一个企业来说,收入就是指企业在销售商品、提供劳务及他人使用本企业资产等日常活动中所形成的经济利益的总流入。它不包括为第三方或客户代收的款项。收入是代表着企业产品和服务的市场反响的一个重要指标。企业应该合理地确认收入,并及时将已经实现的收入入账。以下我们就来详细说明收入是如何确认和计量的。

主营业务收入

1. 销售商品收入

在确认收入时,有几点是必须注意到的。首先,企业必须已将商品所有权上的主要风险和报酬转移给买方。其次,企业既不能保留通常在某种程度上与所有权相联系的继续管理权,也不能保留对已售出商品的有效控制权。再次,与交易相关的经济利益必须能够流入企业,且相关的收入和成本能够可靠地计量。

销售商品的收入应按企业与买方签订的合同或协议的金额或者双方同意的金额来确定。现金折扣在实际发生时应当被确认为当期费用,否则,销售折让在实际发生时就应冲减当期收入。

2. 提供劳务收入

在同一会计年度内开始并完成所提供的劳务,应在劳务完成时确认收入。在计算这项收入时,交易的条件和计量的方法十分重要。会计人员必须确保完成劳务的总收入和总成本能够可靠地计量,并且与交易相关的经济利益能够流入企业。以下为确定劳务完成程度的合宜方法:

- 测量已完成的工作。
- 测量已经提供的劳务占应提供劳务总量的比例,或已发生的成本占估算的总成本之比。
- 确认提供劳务的总收入与合同或协议中规定的金额相符。

其他业务收入

他人使用本企业资产而产生的收入包括包装物出租和出让资产使用权收入。当这些收入按有关合同或协议规定的收费时间和方法进行计量确定时,它们必须满足以下条件:能使交易相关的经济利益流入企业并能够可靠地计量收入的金额。

利息收入

利息收入应按他人使用本企业现金的时间和适用利率计算确定。

7.2　费用

费用可以泛指由企业或个人支付的款项。在会计学意义上,这一术语有两层含义:

- 期间费用。
- 资本性支出、折旧费等间接支出。

为了更好地区分两者，我们使用"费用"和"成本"这两个会计术语。本单元仅探讨期间费用。

费用是指企业在销售商品、提供劳务等日常活动中所产生的经济利益的流出。企业行政管理部门为组织和管理生产经营活动而发生的一般费用和管理费用，财务费用，以及为销售产品和提供劳务而发生的进货费用及销售费用，应当作为期间费用直接计入当期损益。期间费用必须直接在当期利润表中体现出来，冲减收入。

期间费用应在利润表中分项目列示。

（1）销售费用，是指企业在销售商品过程中发生的费用，包括运输费、装卸费、包装费、保险费、展览费和广告费，以及销售机构（含销售网点、售后服务网点等）的职工薪酬及福利费、其他类似工资性质的费用以及业务费等经营费用。商品贸易公司在购买商品过程中所发生的进货费用也包括在内。

（2）管理费用，是指企业为组织和管理企业生产经营活动所发生的费用，包括企业的董事会和行政管理部门的费用、总公司经费（包括行政管理部门职工薪酬、修理费、物料消耗、低值易耗品摊销、办公费和差旅费等）、工会经费、待业保险费、劳动保险费、董事会费、聘请中介机构费、咨询费（含顾问费）、诉讼费、业务招待费、房产税、车船使用税、土地使用税、印花税、技术转让费、矿产资源补偿费、无形资产摊销、职工教育经费、研究与开发费、排污费、存货盘亏或盘盈（不包括应计入营业外支出的存货损失）、计提的坏账准备和存货跌价准备等。

（3）财务费用，是指企业为筹集生产经营所需资金等而发生的费用，包括应当作为期间费用的利息支出（减利息收入）、汇兑损失（减汇兑收益）以及相关的手续费等。

本期支付但应由本期和以后各期负担的费用，应分配计入本期和以后各期。本期尚未支付但应由本期负担的费用，应当计入本期预提费用。

7.3 利润

利润的定义和分类

利润，一般定义为一个企业除去所有的经营费用后所得的回报。然而，会计人员与经济学者计算利润的具体方式却有所不同。经济学者通常将利润视为收入减去机会成本后的所得。在会计学上，利润是指企业在一定期间的经营成果，包括营业利润、投资净利润和营业外净收益。

营业利润等于主营业务收入减去主营业务成本和营业税，加上其他业务利润，减去销售费用、管理费用和财务费用后的金额。

投资净利润是指企业对外投资所取得的收益减去发生的投资损失和计提的投资减值准备后的净额。

营业外净收益是指各种营业外收入扣除营业外支出后的余额。营业外收入和支出与企业的生产经营没有直接的关系。营业外收入包括：固定资产盘盈、处置固定资产净收益、处置无形资产净收益、罚款净收入等。营业外支出包括：固定资产盘亏、处置固定资产净损失、处置无形资产净损失、债务重组损失、无形资产减值准备、固定资产减值准备、在建工程减值准备、罚款支出、捐赠支出、非常损失等。营业外收入和营业外支出应当分别核算，并在利润表中分别列项目反映。

当你查看利润表时，你还会看到另外两个重要的利润：利润总额和净利润。利润总额就是收入减去各项费用，也就是税前净利润。税后净利润则是指扣除了企业所得税后的利润。当这个数值为正数时，我们说企业赚得了利润，反之则处于一种不利的状况。

通常，企业应按月计算利润。如果企业按月计算利润有困难，可以按季或者按年计算利润。如果当期存在收益，则下一步就是要制订利润分配计划。

利润分配

企业当期实现的净利润，加上年初未分配利润（或减去年初未弥补亏损）和其他转入后的余额，为可供分配的利润。它应按下列顺序进行分配：

- 法定盈余公积。
- 任意盈余公积。
- 法律和法规规定的各种公积金。

企业董事会或类似机构建议的利润分配方案，应先列入上报的年度利润分配表，然后提请股东大会或类似机构会议批准。

完成这些顺序后，就可以在投资者间分配利润。首先，给优先股股东分配现金股利。其次是支付普通股股东（现金）股利。最后，再以发行红股的形式增加股本来向普通股股东支付（股票）股利。

经过上述分配后，剩余的利润为未分配利润，可留待以后年度进行分配。

第八单元 资产负债表

8.1 资产负债表的概念

什么是资产负债表？

资产负债表是企业在某一特定时日，通常是在会计年度末财务状况的一个快照。资产负债表之所以被认为是一个"快照"，是因为它给了你一张企业在那个时刻相当清晰的画面，但它本身并没有揭示企业是怎样达到这个状况或者它下一步会怎么样。资产负债表无法包罗万象，你还必须了解来自于其他财务报表的信息，以便从这些数据中获得最大收益。它和利润表一起构成了任何一家企业财务报表的基础。

谁想了解你的资产负债表？

许多个人和组织都会对你公司的财务状况感兴趣。经理、债权人和投资人都需要熟悉公司的资产、负债和所有者权益。你当然想了解你公司的发展还有你谋生的岗位在发生什么。然而，你的债权人也想确保你能够在他们需要的时候把钱还给他们。潜在的投资者也在寻找一个稳定的公司来投资，他们需要财务方面的信息来帮助他们做出合理的决定。你的管理团队需要详细的财务数据，还有工会（如果有的话）也想知道你的雇员是否获得一份公平的收益份额。资产负债表就是一个可以找到所有这些便捷信息的地方。

资产负债表的用途是什么？

当某个人，无论是债权人还是投资者，问你的公司经营状况如何，你当然希望有现成的答案和文件。证明你公司成功的方式就是一份资产负债表。资产负债表是一份你公司在某一特定时点的资产、负债和所有者权益的书面报告。

它是一份累积的记录，反映了自你的公司成立之初起所有的会计事项的记录结果。如果有了正确编制的资产负债表，你就能知道在每一个会计期末你公司的价值是更多了还是更少了，你的债务是更高了还是更低了，你的实收资本是更高了还是更低了。

通过分析你的资产负债表，投资者、债权人和其他人就能估计你公司的偿付能力。资产负债表也可表明资产和负债的结构，债务和权益的相关比例以及你必须留存的收益。所有这些，外部各方都将用来评估你公司的财务状况，这是贷款机构和投资人在他们愿意将资金投入你的公司之前所必须要求的。

8.2 资产负债表的构成

资产负债表包括资产、负债和所有者权益或股东权益。

一般来说，资产负债表被分成两部分是基于以下等式：

$$资产 = 负债 + 所有者权益$$

下面这张简表可以说明资产负债表具体是由哪些部分组成的。

左　边	右　边
资　产	负债及所有者权益
流动资产：包括现金、应收账款、其他相对来说能较快转换为现金的资产	流动负债：包括企业即将在一年内到期的负债
不动产、厂房、设备（固定资产）：企业长期营运资产（减去这些资产的折旧）	非流动负债：一年内不会到期的债务。一个典型例子就是几年内不会到期的已发行债券
无形资产：包括那些自然状态下没有物理形态的长期资产	所有者权益：所有者在企业资产中享有的经济利益
资产总额	负债及所有者权益总额

资产

资产负债表中包括三种类型的资产：流动资产、固定资产和无形资产。

- 流动资产寿命只有一年或更少，这意味着它们能很容易地转换成现金。所有流动资产都是短期的、流动性很高的资产，都能很容易地转换成现金并被用作通货。

- 固定资产也称为长期资产，寿命跨度在一年以上，包括机器、计算机、建筑物和土地等有形资产。固定资产需计算折旧并从资产中扣除。
- 无形资产也是长期资产，如商誉、专利权和著作权等，而这些资产在自然状态下是无形的。

负债

负债在资产负债表的另一边，是企业欠外部客户的经济债务。像资产一样，它们也分为流动负债和非流动负债（即长期负债）。

- 流动负债一般应在一年或一年以内偿付，因此是用流动资产偿付。因为流动资产偿付流动负债，所以两者之间的比率是很重要的：一个企业应当有足够的流动资产来补偿流动负债。
- 非流动负债是当前来看企业所欠的一年以上的债务。

所有者权益

所有者权益（股东权益）是最初投入企业的资金。如果公司决定用税后的净收益再投资于企业，在财务年度结束后，留存收益将从利润表转入到资产负债表中。这两个数字的总和代表的是一个企业的总净值。

所有者权益通常分为三个部分：

- 股本——股份的面值。
- 股本溢价——投资者购买股份时所支付的超出股票面值的金额。
- 留存收益——企业没有分配所留存下来的收益。

为了资产负债表平衡，一边的总资产必须等于另一边的负债加所有者权益。

8.3 如何编制资产负债表

财务报表是向使用者传递有用信息的主要手段，是以日常会计处理的数据和信息为基础，进行再确认的过程。一份完整的资产负债表应包含有以下几个方面。

- 标题

实践中，应用最广泛的标题是资产负债表，但财务状况表也是可行的。如果报告内容包含多个会计期间，则应使用"资产负债表"的复数形式。

- 表首

除了报表名称以外，资产负债表的表首还应当包括公司的注册名称和报表报送的日期。例如：

XYZ 公司

资产负债表

2018 年 12 月 31 日

- 格式

资产负债表有两种基本的编排格式。在账户式下，资产列在报表左边，且总额等于列在报表右边的负债和所有者权益的合计数。另外一种格式叫报告式，即资产列在报告的上面，而紧接着列示的是负债和所有者权益。根据国际惯例，大多数企业采用的是账户式资产负债表。

下面是一个报告式资产负债表的例子。

Alpha 销售公司资产负债表
2018 年 12 月 31 日（已简化）

资产	
流动资产	$2 572
固定资产	$11 111
其他资产	$1 210
资产总计	**$14 893**
负债及所有者权益	
流动负债	$645
长期负债	$4 000
负债合计	**$4 645**
所有者权益	**$10 248**
负债及所有者权益总计	**$14 893**

这是一个账户式资产负债表的例子。

Alpha 销售公司资产负债表
2018 年 12 月 31 日

资产		负债及所有者权益	
流动资产		流动负债	
现金	$695	应付账款	$520
应收账款	$1 237	应付工资	$125
存货	$580	流动负债合计	**$645**
预付保险	$60	非流动负债	
流动资产合计	**$2 572**	应付银行贷款	$4 000
非流动资产		非流动负债合计	**$4 000**
设备	$19 823	负债合计	**$4 645**
减：累计折旧	$8 712	所有者权益	

			(续)
固定资产净值	**$ 11 111**	股本	$ 7 208
专利权	$ 1 210	留存收益	$ 3 040
非流动资产合计	**$ 1 210**	所有者权益合计	**$ 10 248**
资产总计	**$ 14 893**	负债及所有者权益总计	**$ 14 893**

资产负债表的格式可能不同,但它们的编制方法是一样的,具体填列方法如下表所示。

Beta 销售公司资产负债表

2018 年 12 月 31 日

资产		
流动资产		
现金	$×××	根据几个总分类账的余额计算填列,包括库存现金、银行存款和现金等价物
应收票据	$×××	直接根据总分类账的余额填列
应收账款	$×××	根据有关明细分类账的余额计算填列
减:坏账准备	$×××	直接根据总分类账的余额填列
存货	$×××	根据几个总分类账的余额计算填列,包含商品存货、半成品、原材料和日用品等
预付费用	$×××	直接根据总分类账的余额填列
一年内到期的长期债券投资	$×××	根据总分类账和明细分类账的余额分析计算填列
流动资产合计	$×××	
非流动资产		
长期投资	$×××	根据总分类账和明细分类账的余额分析计算填列。这里长期投资总分类账余额应当减去在相关明细分类账中反映的一年内到期的那部分金额
车辆	$×××	
家具	$×××	
设备	$×××	直接根据总分类账的余额填列
建筑物	$×××	
减:累计折旧	$×××	
土地	$×××	
固定资产合计	$×××	
研究和开发	$×××	
专利	$×××	直接根据总分类账的余额填列
版权	$×××	

(续)

非流动资产合计	$×× ×	
资产总计	$×× ×	
负债及所有者权益		
流动负债		
应付账款	$×× ×	根据有关明细分类账的余额计算填列
应付销售税	$×× ×	直接根据总分类账的余额填列
应付工资	$×× ×	
应付短期票据	$×× ×	
应付短期银行贷款	$×× ×	
流动负债合计	$×× ×	
非流动负债		
长期应付票据	$×× ×	根据总分类账和明细分类账的余额分析计算填列。这里长期借款总分类账余额应当减去在相关明细分类账中反映的一年内到期的那部分金额
应付抵押账款	$×× ×	
非流动负债合计	$×× ×	
负债合计	$×× ×	
所有者权益		
股本	$×× ×	直接根据总分类账的余额填列
留存收益	$×× ×	根据有关明细分类账的余额计算填列
所有者权益合计	$×× ×	
负债及所有者权益总计	$×× ×	

第九单元　利　润　表

9.1　利润表的概念

什么是利润表？

利润表也称损益表，是对企业在一定时期（如一个月、三个月或一年）内盈利或亏损的一个总结。利润表记录了企业在这个期间所有的收入和经营费用。它揭示了企业的收益率，而这又反映了企业的经营绩效，以及有多少收益能用于企业的再投资或以分红的形式分配给投资者。

利润表和资产负债表一样都是潜在贷方（如银行、投资者和供应商）所需要的最基本的报表。他们都将以此来决定信用额度。

利润表的用途是什么？

使用利润表是为了追踪企业在一定时期的收入和费用，进而确定企业的经营业绩。小企业主用它来查明企业的哪些地方超出预算而哪些在预算之内。它可以弄清楚那些意外开支的特殊项目，例如电话费、传真费、邮寄费或代理费。同时，利润表可以跟踪产品退货或销售成本占销售额百分比的突然增加，还可以被用来确定企业所得税债务。

9.2 利润表的构成

利润表的常见格式有单步式和多步式。

单步式利润表就是分别计算所有的收入和所有的费用,然后从收入总额中减去费用总额得出净收益。

在单步式中,一个完整的利润表有三个部分:收入、费用和收益。

下面就是典型的单步式利润表。

XYZ 公司利润表
2018 年 12 月 31 日

收入		费用	
净销售额	$50 000	销售费用	$5 000
利息收入	$3 000	管理费用	$3 200
投资收入	$15 000	利息费用	$200
收入合计	**$68 000**	所得税	$3 000
费用		费用合计	**$41 400**
销货成本	$30 000	净利润	**$26 600**

在多步式中,利润表的内容分为多个项目,而这些项目又产生一些中间性信息,并分若干个步骤计算出净收益。为了理解利润表,让我们来详细说明下列基本项目。

净销售额是将所有销售产品或提供服务所产生的总收入减去销售退回、销售折扣或销售折让等。

销货成本是企业用于制造所售产品的费用。它包括公司用于购买生产产品所必需的原材料的花费,以及用于产品制造和人工成本上的花费。

营业费用包括营销费用、工资、租金和研发成本。企业日常经营所发生的任何正常费用都归在这个科目下。

其他收入是非源于企业核心业务的收入。这包括来自于投资、外币兑换的资本利得(或损失),或来源于财产的租金收入等。其中某些收入也可能会定期收到(比如每年的分红),但由于它们是主营业务之外的,所以仍然被认为是其他收入。

非常收入经常和其他收入混在一起,但最好还是能分开来看,因为它是指那些并不会经常发生甚至不是每年都会发生的盈利或亏损。由一次自然灾害引起的费用就是一个例子。

息税前利润在该年企业没有发生其他或非常收入时和营业利润相同。无论如何,息税前利润向投资者表明了一个企业以它在当年所获得的利润支付利息费用(比如债券或银行贷款)的能力。

利息费用是企业必须偿还的欠债金额。它可能是给债券持有人或是给银行。息税前利润减去利息费用等于税前利润。

税金是指所有企业都必须支付的所得税。它通常是所产生的收益的一个百分比，因此每年都会有所变化。

税后净利润是指完税后的利润。对股东而言，税后净利润是一个关键数据，因为它揭示了可分配给股东或为未来增长进行再投资的企业的最终收益。

留存收益是支付股利以后企业所剩的收益。这个金额要么用于企业未来的商业投资，要么为了企业发展而再投资到企业。如果一个企业能分红，则被认为是"收益型"企业；如果它将税后净利润用于企业再投资，则被认为是"成长型"企业。无论是哪种方式，了解企业的政策和目标以确保其净收益是被用于一个满意的方向对投资者而言都是很重要的。

下面是典型的多步式利润表。

XYZ 公司利润表
2018 年 12 月 31 日

净销售额	$50 000	营业费用	
销货成本	$30 000	其他管理费用	$500
销售毛利	**$20 000**	管理费用合计	$3 900
营业费用		营业费用合计	**$7 600**
销售费用		营业利润	**$12 400**
工资薪酬	$2 200	其他收入和利得	
物料消耗	$500	租金收入	$200
折旧费用	$1 000	其他费用和损失	
销售费用合计	$3 700	利息费用	$300
管理费用		税前利润	**$12 300**
工资薪酬	$2 800	所得税	4 920
折旧费用	$600	净利润	**$7 380**

两种格式的利润表都有它们各自的优缺点。单步式简单明了，而多步式能提供更多的信息，并且使用者能从中了解到企业经营成果的不同来源。相对地，这种格式较难理解，会使一些使用者感到困惑。

9.3 如何编制利润表

无论采取哪种方式，利润表都应包含以下内容：

- **标题**

利润表也可称为损益表、收益表或业务经营表，但国际上流行的名称还是利润表。

- **表首**

除了企业名称和财务报表名称"利润表"外，还要明确表明报表所涵盖的期间及所采用的计量单位。

利润表的编制依据是有关收入与费用分类账。与资产负债表不同，利润表是根据收入与费用分类账的发生额（包含累计数）编制的，而资产负债表则根据资产、负债和所有者权益等分类账的余额编制。余额代表某特定时日的剩余金额，而发生额则代表一个会计期间内的流量。总的来说，利润表是建立在下列几个公式的基础之上的。

毛利 = 净销售额 – 销货成本

营业利润 = 毛利 – 营业费用

息税前利润 = 营业利润 + （–）其他收入（损失）+ （–）非常收入（损失）

净利润 = 息税前利润 – 利息费用 – 所得税

留存收益 = 净利润 – 股利

下表是利润表的一个典型样例，具体填列方法如下。

XYZ 公司利润表
2018 年 12 月 31 日

销售收入	来自于向顾客销售所得的收入。根据销售收入分类账的贷方发生额分析填列
销货成本	反映与产品或商品销售收入相关的成本费用。根据销货成本账户的借方发生额分析填列
毛利	也称为总利润，等于销售收入减去销货成本
营业费用	不归于销货成本的所有费用，根据如管理费用、营销费用等分类账的借方发生额分析填列
息税前净利润	在利息和所得税费用入账前的净利润
利息费用	支付公司的未偿债务。根据利息费用分类账的借方发生额分析填列
所得税	应付给政府的费用。根据所得税分类账的借方发生额分析填列
净利润	所有收入减去所有费用后的最终利润

第十单元　现金流量表

10.1　现金流量表的概念

现金流量表是用来分析在特定时间内现金和现金等价物的流入、流出量。目前，现金流量表一般以广义的"现金"作为编制基础。

什么是现金？

现金流量表所关注的只是现金和现金等价物，包括库存现金、银行存款和任何投资到那些短期且流动性高的金融工具上的现金。一般来说，只有那些原定期限不超过三个月的投资才是现金等价物。公认的现金等价物包括短期国库券、商业票据和货币市场基金，这些可以在某个时点转换成现金。接下来我们将会看到，利润的增长不一定意味着更多的现金。

什么是现金流？

现金流简单地说是指一段时期内企业的现金流入和流出。观察现金的流入和流出是业主的主要管理任务之一。现金的流出是根据每月支付的工资、支付给供应商和债权人的支票来衡量的。现金的流入则是你从顾客、债务人和投资者那里收到的现金。

有一些特定的项目在一段时间内可能并不会对你的利润表产生影响,例如:
- 存货购买的大量增加。
- 应收账款的增加。
- 供货商赊销的减少。
- 设备的购买。
- 未被确认的存货减值。
- 银行拒绝续借或延期贷款。
- 债务集中支付。

现金流量表能够以某种利润表无法展现的方式突出这些业务。

谁会关注现金流量表?

主管人员想知道公司所产生的现金是否足够为他们的扩张战略提供资金。

股东想知道公司是否有足够的现金支付股利。

供货商想知道如果提供赊销,他们的顾客是否有购买支付能力。

投资者想对未来的增长潜力进行评估。

雇员则关心他们的雇主为企业经营提供资金保障的整体生存能力如何。

当然银行也想在同意给贷款延期或重新贷款前,通过现金流量表来了解企业是如何使用前期的贷款资金的。

10.2 现金流量表的构成

现金流量表分为三部分,包括以下的内部和外部的来源:
- 经营活动产生的现金流量(内部的)。
- 投资活动产生的现金流量(内部的)。
- 筹资活动产生的现金流量(外部的)。

经营活动产生的现金流量

经营活动通常涉及生产与运输商品以及提供服务。经营活动的现金流量常指的是营运资本,是产生于内部经营的现金流量,是企业销售产品或提供劳务而产生的现金流,是企业真正的活力来源,因为产生于内部,所以是可以控制的。

收到的现金包括:
- 出售商品或提供劳务。
- 利息收入。
- 分红收入。

支付的现金包括:
- 购买存货。
- 工资。
- 税款和利息费用。

- 其他（公用事业费用、租金等）。

投资活动产生的现金流量

投资活动包括的各种交易和事项涉及证券（不包括现金等价物）、土地、建筑物、设备和其他一般不以再销售为持有目的的资产的购买和销售，也包括贷款的发放和收回。投资活动不像经营活动那样分类，因为它们和企业主要的、正在进行的经营活动（通常是销售商品和提供劳务）没有直接的关系。

收到的现金包括：

- 固定资产的销售。
- 企业分立部分的销售。
- 出售投资于其他企业的股票或债券（现金等价物除外）。
- 对其他企业的贷款本金的收回。

支付的现金包括：

- 购买固定资产。
- 购买其他企业的股票和债券（现金等价物除外）。
- 对其他企业的贷款。

筹资活动产生的现金流量

所有的筹资活动处理的是企业所有者（权益筹资）和债权人（债务筹资）的现金流量。例如，发行股票或债券的现金收入都将列示在筹资活动下。同样地，回购股票（库存股）、赎回债券以及股利的支付也都属于筹资活动。

收到的现金包括：

- 发行本企业的股票。
- 借款（债券、票据、抵押等）。

支付的现金包括：

- 股东的分红。
- 偿还借款本金。
- 回购本企业的股票（库存股）。

10.3 如何编制现金流量表

下面是现金流量表的基本格式。

现金流量表	
经营活动产生的现金流量	$×× ×
投资活动产生的现金流量	$×× ×
筹资活动产生的现金流量	$×× ×
现金净增加（减少）额	$×× ×

(续)

现金流量表	
现金期初余额	$×××
现金期末余额	$×××

企业经营活动产生的现金流量就是那些与利润表项目直接相关的现金流入和流出。但是由于利润表的编制基础为权责发生制，其本身并不能反映经营活动中的现金流量，因此，需要将权责发生制调整为现金收付制。调整的方法有两种：直接法和间接法。虽然两者产生的结果是一样的，但是间接法更常用一些，因为它调和了由经营活动提供的净收益和净现金流量之间的差别。

间接法

间接法受到欢迎是因为这种方法相对而言要简单些。间接法从净利润（来自于利润表）开始，帮你将那些不影响现金流的项目从权责发生制调整到现金收付制。下面是计算公式。

经营活动的现金流量 =

净利润（注：直接来自于利润表）

+ 不影响现金流的**费用或损失**

+ **流动资产的减少**与**流动负债的增加**

− 不影响现金流的**收入和利得**

− **流动资产的增加**与**流动负债的减少**（注：在确定此项时，流动资产的增加不包括现金或现金等价物）

下面是用间接法编制现金流量表的例子。

ABC 公司现金流量表

2018 年 12 月 31 日

经营活动产生的现金流量	
净利润①	$207 901
加项（现金的来源）	
折旧	$130 900
应付账款的增加	$12 034
应计所得税的增加	$41 500
减项（现金的使用）	
应收账款的增加	$111 800
存货的增加	−$95 300
经营活动产生的现金流量净额	**$375 835**
投资活动产生的现金流量	
设备	−$104 200
投资活动产生的现金流量净额	**−$104 200**

（续）

筹资活动产生的现金流量	
应付票据	$400 000
筹资活动产生的现金流量净额	**$400 000**
现金净增加额	**$671 635**

① 净利润直接来自于利润表。

直接法

直接法不是从已报告的净利润开始，而是分析经营活动的不同类型，计算每一项引起的现金流量的总和。直接法在计算之前，所有的权责发生制账户都必须先转换成现金数字。

这张工作表能够帮助解释直接法现金流量表中的金额是怎样确定的。

A. 来自于顾客的现金收入		
	净销售额	$××
	加：应收账款的期初余额	$××
	减：应收账款的期末余额	$××
	来自于顾客的现金收入	$××
B. 为存货支付的现金		
	加：存货的期末余额	$××
	减：存货的期初余额	$××
	加：应付账款的期初余额	$××
	减：应付账款的期末余额	$××
	为存货支付的现金	$××
C. 为营业费用支付的现金		
	营业费用	$××
	减：折旧费用	$××
	加：预付费用的期末余额	$××
	减：预付费用的期初余额	$××
	加：应付费用的期初余额	$××
	减：应付费用的期末余额	$××
	为营业费用支付的现金	$××
D. 为利息费用支付的现金		
	利息费用	$××
	加：应付利息的期初余额	$××
	减：应付利息的期末余额	$××
	为利息费用支付的现金	$××

(续)

E. 为企业所得税支付的现金

	所得税	$×× ×
	加：应交税金的期初余额	$×× ×
	减：应交税金的期末余额	$×× ×
	为企业所得税支付的现金	$×× ×

下面是直接法下现金流量表的例子。

XYZ公司现金流量表
2018年12月31日

经营活动产生的现金流量	
来自于顾客的现金收入	$1 342 500
为存货支付的现金	$392 266
为营业费用支付的现金	$300 000
为利息费用支付的现金	$70 000
为企业所得税支付的现金	$204 399
经营活动产生的现金流量净额	**$375 835**
投资活动产生的现金流量	
设备销售收入	$346 800
购买设备	$451 000
投资活动产生的现金流量净额	**-$104 200**
筹资活动产生的现金流量	
长期贷款	$400 000
长期债务的减少	$1 282 500
筹资活动产生的现金流量净额	**-$882 500**
现金净增加（减少）额	**-$610 865**

Appendix III

专业词汇表

A

abbreviated	*adj.* 简短的
accelerated depreciation	加速折旧法
account number	科目代码
accountant	*n.* 会计（员），会计师
accounting element	会计要素
accounting entity	会计主体
accounting period	会计期间
accounting practice	会计核算
accrual basis	权责发生制
accrued expense	预提费用，应计费用
additional	*adj.* 另外的
addition	*n.* 加，增加，附加
administration	*n.* 管理，行政部门
administrative cost	管理费用
advances from customer	预收客户款
after-sales services network	售后服务网点
algebraical	*adj.* 代数的
allocation	*n.* 分配
allowance	*n.* 销售折让
amortization	*n.* 摊销
amortize	*v.* 摊销
annual	*adj.* 每年的
anticipate	*vt.* 预期，预料
applied	*adj.* 应用的，实用的
appropriate	*adj.* 适当的
arbitrarily	*adv.* 武断地，任意地，专横地
assessed value	评估价
asset	*n.* (*pl*) 资产
assumption	*n.* 假定
at a premium or discount	溢价或折价
attributable	*adj.* 可归于……的

B

Babylon	n. 巴比伦
bankrupt	v. 破产
bankruptcy	n. 破产
be converted into	被转换成……
be taken into consideration	被考虑进来
bearer bond	不记名债券
beaver pelt	海狸毛皮
bias	n. 偏见，偏爱
bill of lading	提货单
board of directors	董事会
bondholder	n. 债券持有人
bonds investment	债券投资
bonus	n. 奖金
book value	账面价值
bookkeeper	n. 簿记员
bookkeeping	n. 簿记
boundary	n. 边界，分界线
budget	n. 预算
bulked	a. 巨大的，重要的
by coincidence	巧合地

C

callable bond	可提前（可通知）偿还的债券
capital expenditure	资产支出
capital gain	资本利得
capital lease	融资租赁
capital reserve	资本公积
cash basis	现金收付制
cash equivalent	现金等价物
cash in the bank	银行存款
cash on hand	库存现金
category	n. 种类
characteristics	n. 特征
Chart of Account Title	会计科目表

C

(续)

英文	中文
checkbook	n. 支票簿
chronologically	adv. 序时地
claim	n. 债权，索赔
closing cost	记账成本
collateral	n. 抵押品
columnar	adj. 分纵栏印刷或书写的
commercial paper	商业本票
commodities	n. 日用品
common share	普通股（股份）
common stock	普通股
component	n. 成分
(be) comprised of	构成，由……组成
consistently	adv. 一贯地，始终如一地
consolidated financial statement	合并会计报表
consulting	adj. 咨询的
contingent	adj. 因（情况）而变的，看……而定的
contingent liability	或有负债
contractual interest rate	息票利率
contribute	vt. 分配
convertible bond	可转换债券
copyright	n. 版权
corporation	n. 公司，股份公司
corresponding	adj. 相应的
cost method	成本法
credit	n. 贷方
creditor	n. 债权人
criteria	n. 标准
currency	n. 通货，货币
current assets	流动资产
current ratio	流动比率
current year profits	本年利润

APPENDIX

D

debit	*n.* 借方
debt financing	债务筹资
debt securities	债务证券
debt to total asset ratio	资产负债比
declining rate on cost method	成本递减法
deduct	*v.* 减除,扣除
deferred assets	递延资产
deferred income tax	递延收入税
depreciation	*n.* 折旧
(be) derived from	得自,由来
designated	*adj.* 指定的
devotion	*n.* 投入
differentiate	*vt.* 发行,发售
discretionary surplus reserve	法定公益金
dispose	*v.* 处置
diversify	*v.* 多元化
dividend split	股票分割
dividends payable	应付股利
domestic	*adj.* 国内的
donation	*n.* 捐赠品,捐款,贡献
Double-declining balance method	双倍余额递减法
drawing up	草拟

E

earnings	*n.* 收益,利润
Earnings before Interest and Tax (EBIT)	息税前利润
educe	*vt.* 得出,导出
effective interest method	实际利率法
effective interest rate	实际利率
eliminate	*v.* 撤销
embody	*vt.* 具体表达 *v.* 包含
endowment insurance	养老保险
entertainment expenses	业务招待费
entitle	*vt.* 给……权利
entity	*n.* 实体

E

(续)

equity financing	权益筹资
equity method	权益法
equity securities	权益证券
excavation	n. 开发
executive	n. 执行者,经理主管人员
extend loan	延期贷款,债务集中支付
extraordinary income	税后净利润

F

face value	票面价值
finance expenses	财务费用
faciliate	促进,帮助
financial position	财务状况
financing	n. 筹措资金,融资
fixed percentage on declining base amount method	固定比率折旧法
for the purpose of	以……为目的的
foreclose	vi. 取消赎回权
foreign currency	外币
foreseeable	adj. 可预知的
franchise	n. 特许权
fraud	n. 欺诈行为
freight	n. 运输
freight charge	运输费
frequently-occurring	经常发生的
fundamental	adj. 基础的　n. 基本面

G

gain on disposal	处置利得
give rise to	引起,使发生
gear	n. 齿轮
general and administrative expenses	管理费用
general ledger	总分类账
general partnership	普通合伙制
generate	vt. 产生
going concern	持续经营
goodwill	n. 商誉
gross profit	利润总额,毛利润

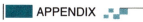

G

(续)

growth orientated	成长型
guaranteed dividend	有保证的股利

H

handcrafted	*adj.* 手工的，手工艺的
handling fee	装卸费
highlight	*vt.* 突出

I

identical	*adj.* 同样的
identify	*v.* 识别，鉴定
illustrate	*vt.* 举例说明
impairment	*n.* 损害，损伤
in conformity with	与……一致
inappropriate profit	未分配利润
income orientated	收益型
income tax	所得税
incur	*v.* 产生
indicator	*n.* 指示器
inevitably	*adv.* 不可避免地
innovator	*n.* 改革者
insignificant	*adj.* 不重要的
installment	*n.* 分期付款
intangible assets	无形资产
interest rate stated on bonds	债券的名义利率
interest revenue	利息收入
interim	*n.* 期间
inventory	*n.* 物品清单，库存
investee	*n.* 被投资者
investor	*n.* 投资者
(be) involved in	涉及，专心
issue	*v.* 发行
insurance	*n.* 保险费
(to) issue capital stock	发行股票

J

joint-stock company	股份公司
journal	*n.* 日记账

L

label	vt. 标注　n. 标签
ledger	n. 分类账
legal entity	法人实体
lessee	n. 承租方
lessor	n. 出租方
liability	n. 负债
lifeblood	n. 生命必需的血液，活力的源泉
limited partnership	有限责任合伙制
liquidated	adj. 清算的
liquidation	n. 清算
liquidity	n. 流动性，偿债能力
litigation	n. 诉讼，起诉
loan	n. 贷款
long-term investment	长期投资
loss on disposal	处置损失

M

management result	经营成果
manifest	adj. 显然的，明白的
manufacturer	n. 制造业者，厂商
market interest rate	市场利率
market value	市场价
matured	adj.（票据等）到期的
maturity	n.（票据）到期
merge	vi. 合并
meticulous	adj. 小心翼翼的
minus sign	减号
misconduct	n. 不正当的行为
mis-specified	入错账
money market funds	货币市场基金
money measurement assumption	货币计量假设
monopolistic	adj. 垄断的
mortgage	n. 抵押
moving away	离开
multiple-step form	多步式
multiply	v. 相乘

N

State Intellectual Property Office	国家知识产权局
net investment profit	投资净收益
net non-operating income	营业外收支净额
net profit	净利润
Net Profit after Taxes (NPAT)	税后净利润
net revenue	净收益
nominal ledger	名义分类账
nomination	n. 提名
notes payable	应付票据

O

obligation	n. 债务
observe	vt. 遵守
obsolescence	n. 过时,老化
offer	vt. 出售 n. 报价
operating expense	营业费用
operating lease	经营租赁
operating profit	营业利润
operating result	业务成果,运营结果
opportunity cost	机会成本
option	n. 选择
original	adj. 最初的,原始的
other operating revenue	其他业务收入
outlay	n. 费用
owners' equity	所有者权益
ownership	n. 所有权

P

packaging	n. 包装
par (face) value	票面价值
parent company	母公司
patent	n. 专利
payroll	n. 薪水册
penalty	n. 处罚,罚款
periodic expense	期间费用

P

(续)

permanent	*adj.* 持久的
perspicuous	*adj.* 明白的,明了的
physical token	自然代币
(to) play a great role in	在……方面起重要作用
pledge	*v.* 保证
(to) plow all of its earnings back	以收益作为资本投资
plumbing	*n.* 管道设备
posting	过账
preferred stock	优先股
prescribe	*v.* 指示,规定
prescribed	*adj.* 规定的
present	*v.* 呈现,显示
presentation	*n.* 介绍,陈述,表达
principal	本金
property	*n.* 财产
proportion	*n.* 比例
proprietor	*n.* 所有者,经营者
provision	*n.* 供应,预备
provision for expenses	预提费用
pull	*n.* 影响力
purchase order	采购单

Q

quotation	*n.* 引用语,报价

R

rationally	*adv.* 理性地
real estate brokers' commission	房地产经纪人佣金
rebate	*n.* 销售折扣
receipt	*n.* 收据
reconcile	*vt.* 使和解,使和谐
redeem	*vt.* 赎回,偿还
registered bond	记名债券
relate	*v.* 与……联系,与……有关

R

(续)

relevant	*adj.* 相应的
reliably	*adv.* 可靠地
remainder	*n.* 剩余部分
remise	*vt.* 让与
Renaissance	*n.* 文艺复兴时期
render	*v.* 提供
rendering of service	提供劳务
rental	*n.* 租金收入
representative	*n.* 代表
respectively	*adv.* 分别地
restrictive	*adj.* 限制性的
retain	*vt.* 留存
revenue	*n.* 收入
revenue expenditure	营业支出
reverse	*adj.* 相反,反面
risk-immune	没有风险的

S

sales invoice	销售发票
sales volume	销售量
salvage value	残值
secured bond	担保债券
security	*n.* (*pl*) 有价证券
segment	*n.* 分割
sequence	*n.* 次序,顺序,序列
serial bond	分期还本债券
service life	服务年限
Service-life Method	平均年限法
severance pay	解雇费,员工安置费
shareholder	*n.* 股东
shares investment	股票投资
short-term loans payable	应付短期借款
simultaneously	*adv.* 同时地
single-step form	单步式
sizing up	判断

S

(续)

slash	*vt.* 暴跌
soar	*v.* 暴涨（指股票）
sole proprietorship	独资（经营）制
solid	*adj.* 可靠的，可信赖的
sophisticated	*adj.* 久经世故的
specify	*v.* 规定
stake	*n.* 赌金，奖品
statute	*n.* 法令，条例
statutory surplus reserve	法定盈余公积
stipulate	*v.* 规定，保证
storage	*n.* 贮藏，存储
straight-line method	直线摊销法
subsidiary (affiliated) company	子（附属）公司
subsidiary ledger	明细分类账
substantial	*adj.* 大量的，实质的，真实的
subtraction	*n.* 减少
sum-of-years'-digits method	年数总和法
supervision	*n.* 监督，管理
surplus reserve	盈余公积
suspend	*vt.* 推迟

T

T-account	T形账户
tangible	*adj.* 有形的
tangible asset	有形资产
term bond	定期债券
the Materiality Principle	重要性原则
the Prudence Principle	谨慎性原则
the Realization Principle	实质重于形式原则
tightness	*n.* 紧缩
times interest earned ratio	已获利息倍数
total output	总产量
trademark	*n.* 商标
trade-offs	交易
transportation tax	车船使用税
treasury bill	国库券
treasury stock	库存股份

U

undesirable	*adj.* 不受欢迎的
undistributed profit retained	未分配利润
union dues	工会经费
Unit-of-Production Method	产量法
unsecured bond	无担保债券
usage	*n.* 使用，用法
useful life	使用年限

V

vary	*v.* 变化
vendor	*n.* 厂商
venture capital	风险资本
viability	*n.* 生存能力
vital	*adj.* 至关重要的
voting right	表决权

W

wear and tear	损坏，破裂
welfare	*n.* 福利
withdrawal	*n.* 收回，撤销
with regard to	关于
working capital	营运资本
worksheet	*n.* 工作底稿
wrap page	包装材料

参 考 文 献

[1] 韦安特. 会计学原理 [M]. 北京：中信出版社，2002.
[2] 李惠. 会计专业英语 [M]. 北京：高等教育出版社，2000.
[3] 李爽. 会计英语 [M]. 北京：中国财政经济出版社，1996.
[4] 陈汉东. 实用会计英语 [M]. 长沙：湖南人民出版社，1999.
[5] 叶建芳，孙红星. 会计英语 [M]. 上海：上海财经大学出版社，2003.
[6] 于久洪. 会计英语 [M]. 北京：中国人民大学出版社，2005.
[7] 侯立新. 会计英语 [M]. 北京：机械工业出版社，2006.
[8] 郝绍伦. 会计英语导航 [M]. 合肥：中国科学技术大学出版社，2003.
[9] 吴冰. 会计英语基础教程 [M]. 北京：北京大学出版社，2005.
[10] 黄世忠，陈箭深，等. 会计英语教程 [M]. 厦门：厦门大学出版社，1991.
[11] 李越科. 会计英语简明教程 [M]. 成都：西南财经大学出版社，2005.
[12] 常勋，萧华. 会计专业英语 [M]. 3版. 上海：立信会计出版社，2004.
[13] 聂萍. 现代会计英语 [M]. 长沙：湖南人民出版社，2003.
[14] 中华人民共和国财政部. 企业会计制度 [S]. 北京：经济科学出版社，2001.
[15] 中华人民共和国财政部. 企业会计准则 [S]. 北京：经济科学出版社，2006.
[16] 郭葆春. 会计专业英语 [M]. 北京: 中国人民大学出版社，2016.
[17] 严郁. 会计专业英语 [M]. 北京: 中国人民大学出版社，2015.
[18] Kieso，DonaldE. Fundamentals of Intermediate Accounting [M]. New York: John Wiley & Sons，2006.
[19] John J Wild，Ken Shaw，Barbara Chiappetta. Fundamental Accounting Principles [M]. Beijing：McGraw – Hill Education（Asia）Co and China Renmin University Press，2007.